LONDON'S CLASSIC
RESTAURANTS

LONDON'S CLASSIC
RESTAURANTS

Cara Frost-Sharratt

Interlink Books

First American edition published in 2011 by

INTERLINK BOOKS
An imprint of Interlink Publishing Group, Inc.
46 Crosby Street, Northampton, Massachusetts 01060
www.interlinkbooks.com

Library of Congress Cataloging-in-Publication Data available
ISBN 978-1-56656-851-7

Commissioning Editor: Emma Pattison
Designer: Lucy Parissi
Production: Marion Storz
Cartography: William Smuts

Printed and bound in Singapore

To request our complete 48-page full-color catalog, please call us toll free at 1-800-238-LINK,
visit our website at www.interlinkbooks.com, or send us an e-mail: info@interlinkbooks.com

CONTENTS

INTRODUCTION

If you study any culture in the world you will discover that food has an extremely important role to play in all aspects of people's lives. From family gatherings, celebrations and festivals, to times of hardship or war, it is food that helps to define who we are, where we live and the links we have with our forebears. In fact, food is such an intrinsic part of everyday life that it is the one thing that truly unites people all over the world.

Food, Glorious Food

At its most fundamental, food is essential for our survival. When hunters and gatherers first learnt how to differentiate wholesome plants from those that were poisonous and became adept at tracking and killing wild animals, food was very much a necessity; nothing more than a tool for the survival and continuation of the human race. And yet, meals would have still provided the opportunity to relax and socialise with the group, to indulge in the pleasure of having a full stomach and a chance to rest before setting off on the next foray into the wild. It could therefore be argued that restaurants are as old as food itself. If we take all the elements we consider important for a memorable meal out, the basics don't differ that much from the anticipation and enjoyment of a meal thousands of years ago.

The Evolution of the Restaurant

The phenomenon of paying for a meal in a restaurant can be traced way back to the ninth and tenth centuries when eating out was a popular pastime for people living in China, as well as across the Roman and Islamic world. The concept arrived in the West a little later on but with no less gusto and restaurants were springing up all over France, Spain, Portugal and England

throughout the eighteenth century. Coffee houses and taverns existed for a long time before, but these mainly served a rough and ready set dish and were generally the preserve of men. London has always been an important trading route as well as a major world city and, as such, it has traditionally been home to a large number of restaurants. Traders, sailors, businessmen, travelling show people and artisans all needed places where they could buy a meal and a drink and restaurants were there to cater to their requirements.

As restaurants became more commonplace in London, they also began to differentiate themselves. There was a greater choice on restaurant menus and there were specialist restaurants, as well as those catering to differing budgets. So, working class factory workers might treat themselves to pie and mash at M. Manze (see page 104) on a Saturday lunchtime, while the gentry would take a table at Rules (see page 95) to sample the best that the new hunting season had to offer. London is set apart from other cities because of the sheer diversity and number of restaurants that it is home to. Every area of the city, no matter how small or tucked away, has its own much-loved restaurants with loyal regulars. Restaurants demarcate an area but they also help to unite the city. Word soon spreads when a good restaurant opens its doors and people will come flocking from all over the capital to dine there.

Dining Out in London

Restaurants help to unify and define London, from the smallest café to the grandest hotel restaurant with international acclaim. It has always been a melting pot of different cultures and nationalities and restaurants have been at the forefront of reflecting this diversity. A restaurant often has the dual purpose of providing sustenance as well as a dose of nostalgia: an authentic taste of home for those living or travelling in London. Today, it is possible to dine out on food from virtually every corner of the globe somewhere in London and the restaurant scene continues to reflect the wonderfully diverse nature of the city.

London has built up a worldwide reputation for the quality of its restaurants over the years and this spans all cuisines and all calibre of establishment. With literally thousands of eateries in the capital, it is no mean feat to be considered a classic London restaurant. So many criteria must be fulfilled in order to be considered worthy of an entry in the 'classic' list that few establishments are eligible. However, this book attempts to bring together some of the oldest, best-loved, most enduring and relevant eateries in London. You will find five-star hotel restaurants nestling up next to venerable coffee shops and long-established French bistros. Price, location and awards are irrelevant here: what matters is the restaurant's ability to serve extraordinary food in convivial settings.

Where to go if you like...

Romance

Michelin Stars

Fine Wine

Sumptuous Décor

History

Food in a Hurry

Celebrity Spotting

SOHO AND FITZROVIA

These two adjoining areas couldn't be more different. Soho is one of the major nightlife centres of London, whilst the more staid and stately Fitzrovia donates a greater proportion of its streets to office and residential usage. However, the entire area is teeming with bars, cafes and restaurants catering to every possible taste and the sheer numbers involved have forced many inferior establishments out and others to up their game. With the bohemian history of Fitzrovia and the reputation of Soho as the media hub of London, it is no great surprise that clandestine meetings and boozy business lunches are still a regular occurrence at restaurants such as The Gay Hussar, and The French House.

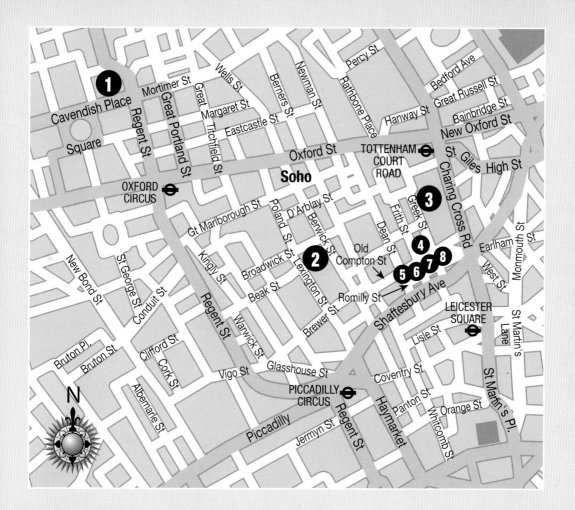

1. The Langham
2. Andrew Edmunds
3. The Gay Hussar
4. Bar Italia
5. The French House
6. Patisserie Valerie
7. Kettner's
8. Maison Bertaux

Andrew Edmunds

46 Lexington Street, W1

Despite serving meals to appreciative diners for over 20 years, Andrew Edmunds doesn't rest on its laurels and it is this attention to detail that ensures it remains top of many people's list of favourite London eateries.

This restaurant isn't particularly big or even particularly well known outside of London – perhaps even Soho – but it certainly justifies its place as one of London's classic restaurants. Once people have stumbled across this tiny little shop front on Lexington Street, they seem to fall madly in love with it and return again and again.

The first visit tends to be through a personal recommendation or perhaps a review and, as with all first-time eating experiences, there is a sense of trepidation. However, as soon as you have tucked into the first mouthful of the starter, all that uncertainty falls away and you can succumb to the enjoyment of the food and atmosphere in the knowledge that you are in safe hands. Such is the comforting feeling that one experiences when dining in Andrew Edmunds. It is a wonderful combination of the food, the intimacy of the dining room and the individuality of the venue itself.

There are actually two dining areas, as the restaurant has a basement, and both of these are usually packed to bursting at busy times. It is quite hard to fathom how they manage to fit so many diners into such a compromising space and yet, instead of putting people off, this seems to have them flocking back. As the whole restaurant provides an intimate setting, it doesn't feel as if too many people are being accommodated and Andrew Edmunds actually works equally well for a business meeting or a romantic dinner. This tucked away and discreet eatery is ideal for extended lunches and the restaurant acts as a bolthole from the busy London streets just a short distance from its door.

The food is largely based around Mediterranean flavours, with a menu that changes daily, whilst keeping some classic dishes on the list permanently. This has the benefit of encouraging regulars to return. It appeals to those who choose a restaurant based on a favourite dish as well as people who favour the atmosphere but wish to diversify their lunch choices. The wine list is heralded as one of the best in the business because of the care taken with regards to variety and price point. Staff are knowledgeable enough to help diners make informed choices on wines that would best complement their food.

The restaurant itself is quirky, if unremarkable, and it has achieved a select status without throwing its weight around. The passion behind the cooking and the quality of the ingredients speak volumes about the integrity of the place and this is why people keep returning. In a world of big, brash restaurants with clinical, conveyor-belt style efficiency, Andrew Edmunds has kept its soul and genuine food lovers can spot this a mile off.

Bar Italia

22 Frith Street, W1

The authenticity of Bar Italia is present in its décor, its menu and even its staff. You can step off the streets of Soho and, once inside, feel as if you are right in the heart of Italy.

If eateries could talk then Bar Italia would certainly have a few tales to tell. This unassuming Soho hangout has been serving coffee and pizza from its Frith Street premises since 1949. As a 24-hour café in the heart of the capital's traditional Red Light district, the clientele is diverse, to say the least. Media workers pop in for take-outs in the morning, people watchers jostle for space at the limited number of pavement tables throughout the day, whilst clubbers and night owls pack the place out from dusk until dawn.

Not many cafés can make claim to the success and longevity that Bar Italia enjoys. It is without doubt a Soho institution, which is fondly regarded by its patrons, whether they are tourists or regulars. Its real charm lies in its authenticity and its unpretentious, shabby chic styling. Whilst millions of pounds are spent on the interiors of neighbouring bars and clubs, Bar Italia simply scrubs its worn-looking floor tiles and polishes its authentic retro furnishings. It proves that reputation and reliability are far more important than sleek makeovers when it comes to the staying power of a café or restaurant. Bar Italia has seen hundreds of establishments come and go over the years and yet it has managed to more than hold its own against the competition by being a constant presence in a rapidly changing area of London. The authenticity of Bar Italia is present in its décor, its menu and even its staff. You can step off the streets of Soho and, once inside, feel as if you are right in the heart of Italy.

Soho squashes and squeezes itself into one square mile and the majority of streets are lined with restaurants, bars, clubs and cafés. With so many establishments vying for the attention and the wallets of the discerning passers-by, it's no mean feat to stay in business for as long as Bar Italia has. From the Teddy Boys, Mods and Rockers of the fifties and sixties, to the punks and drag queens of the eighties and nineties, this humble café has served them all over the years.

The menu has no aspirations towards culinary greatness: it is basic Italian fare served with Italian flair. But that's not what makes Bar Italia a classic London restaurant. It has proven its worth by standing the test of time and appealing to different generations without resorting to gimmicks, flashy furniture or pretentious food. By changing nothing, Bar Italia has kept its essence intact and it hasn't sold its soul. Long may it reign over Soho.

The French House

49 Dean Street, W1

The French House is an eating and drinking experience that has been stripped back to its essential parts, allowing people to interact without the intrusions of modern society.

This bar and restaurant is a Soho gem with a tumultuous history that began when the bar was a gin parlour in the mid-nineteenth century. The French House doesn't have any lofty pretensions and instead is more like a second home to its doggedly loyal patrons. Over the years, it has been a haven for numerous writers, thespians and poets who have been drawn here by the convivial atmosphere and the opportunity for anonymity inside the modestly sized rooms.

Like many successful Soho institutions that have survived the Wars and the transience of London's eating and drinking trends, The French House has undergone a number of name changes and proprietor changes. However, it has never altered its basic principles and these are the key to its

sustained popularity. By continuing to go against the trends and gizmos of modern watering holes, The French House has stayed loyal to its founding beliefs and its customers have stayed loyal to the establishment. You won't find monster-sized television screens or fruit machines in the bar, mobile phones are banned inside and conversation is encouraged, free from the warbling of tinny background music. Essentially, The French House is an eating and drinking experience that has been stripped back to its essential parts, allowing people to interact without the intrusions of modern society.

The restaurant is upstairs from the bar and the fare is pared-down, wholesome plates of food that will put a smile on your face. This certainly isn't fancy dining but that's not what makes The French House a classic restaurant. This is a restaurant that people rely on for a tummy full of comfort food that has been cooked to perfection: dishes such as fillet steak, Scottish salmon, and creamy dauphinoise potatoes. These are heartfelt dishes served with love and lashings of rich, luscious sauces. The restaurant is gloriously free of pretentiousness, which is both an honest and refreshing take on the whole dining experience. People don't always want to be bombarded with ingredients or dishes they have never heard of. Often, they simply want to conjure up food memories and choose a particular restaurant based on its ability to wrap them up in a comfort blanket of foodie heaven.

The French House has been doing this successfully for years and patrons really are treated like family members. Both the bar and the restaurant are constantly humming with the sing-song rhythms of animated conversation. There is an extensive list of wine and Champagne that is served by the glass. This negates the need to pay for and gulp down gallons of unwanted alcohol, or be pushed into a second or third choice wine based on its availability in a single serving. The French House has also stood its ground when it comes to lager. A rarity in British pub terms, it doesn't serve pints and instead only serves lager in half pint glasses.

Such idiosyncrasies have only served to endear it further to its customers and have clarified its position as a truly unique venue. By refusing to fit the mould and follow the crowd The French House has quietly gone about its business and attended to the needs of its customers. In return, they show their appreciation by flocking here for a leisurely drink, some meaningful conversation and a hearty meal and they will continue to do so ad infinitum.

The Gay Hussar

2 Greek Street, W1

The Gay Hussar is as much a Soho institution as a restaurant. To call it simply a restaurant doesn't go anywhere near encapsulating the great part it has had to play in the recent history of the area.

The Gay Hussar has been serving traditional Hungarian food from its Soho premises since 1953. It is perhaps a little strange then that the man who set up the restaurant and was its proprietor for 34 years had a Swiss father and a Welsh mother. And yet, in London restaurant terms this is inconsequential; a quirky fact that only adds to the likeability of the place. Victor Sassie was certainly no stranger to Hungarian food and culture, having spent time in Budapest during the war. However, why his passion for the cuisine led him to dedicate a restaurant towards its endeavour is something that only he would have been able to answer. Regardless of the tenuous links of the original owner to the food's country of origin, there was no disputing the authenticity of the menu and classic dishes are still enjoyed by customers from all over the world.

With its location in the heart of media London, The Gay Hussar earned itself a reputation as a luncheon bolt-hole for journalists, editors and politicians who would gather for crisis talks and to exchange top-secret information and juicy gossip.

Although the food and wine in The Gay Hussar is based around Hungarian cuisine, there are no hard and fast rules. Big plates of rich, tasty food emerge from the kitchen and the classic flavours of paprika, red cabbage and beetroot permeate many of the dishes. You will spot many classic recipes on the menu, such as goulash, and stuffed cabbage, as well as other more modern takes on typical dishes, showing off the Chef's skill at re-interpreting the food. A good selection of Hungarian wine is available to offer more authenticity to the dining experience and, although not widely appreciated for their wine-making skills, Hungarian tipples are highly praised by those in the know.

The Gay Hussar is as much a Soho institution as a restaurant. To call it simply a restaurant doesn't go anywhere near encapsulating the great part it has had to play in the recent history of the area. The people who have dined here and the legacy they have left, have all added up to create a unique and fascinating cubby hole that is positively brimming over with character.

The interior of the restaurant is an anachronism in the heart of über-modern Soho. The dark wood walls are decorated with caricatures of political figures, whilst the bookshelves are lined with memoirs and dusty old political tomes that have no chance of being stolen – but maybe that's the idea.

The compact interior is just large enough to accommodate two rows of tables along the walls. During peak times, the space in the middle turns into a veritable rabbit run, along which busy waiting staff vie for diners' attention above the din of exuberant voices. Plates are precariously balanced on well-practised arms and the service is smooth and slick. It is an environment that hardly seems conducive to serious political discussion. However, if you venture upstairs you will discover another two floors and these house the private dining rooms where covert conversations and meetings have been conducted over the years.

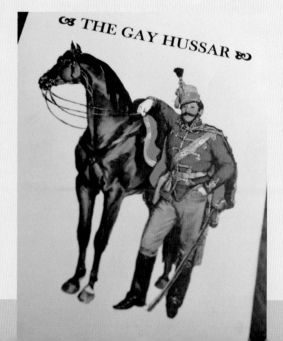

Kettner's

29 Romilly Street, W1

Kettner's is the kind of restaurant where you can get dressed up to the nines for a glass of bubbly in the famous Champagne Bar, or slip into something more comfortable for a bite to eat in The Brasserie.

Kettner's has been serving patrons in its opulent dining rooms since 1867. It has recently undergone an extensive refurbishment and a complete menu overhaul. Prior to this, Kettner's was a stylish pizza restaurant. First-time visitors would often walk in, looking confused because they thought they had arrived at the wrong restaurant. It was certainly the poshest pizza place in town and it gave diners on a budget the chance to eat out in style.

In its new guise, the menu is all about upmarket brasserie style dishes. The interior has been given a huge injection of understated glamour, with beautiful parquet flooring, voluminous, airy rooms overflowing with Victorian design features and classic furnishings and table settings. This is a truly elegant collection of interconnecting spaces that can accommodate drinkers, diners and revellers in equal measure. Kettner's prides itself on catering to every dining requirement from the office lunch or the pre-theatre bite, through to the long, leisurely evening meal. There has always been a cheeky sense of irony and fun at Kettner's and this certainly hasn't been lost in the revamp. The wonderfully

decadent Pudding Bar is quite literally a long, marble bar on which are displayed a mouth-watering variety of sweet treats. Even the most hardened savoury palate will be swayed by the indulgence of a whole room dedicated to desserts. Those with a sweet tooth have no hope of abstaining. The Pudding Bar is open until late so the timing of your sugar-hit requirement is irrelevant.

Kettner's has always captured the hearts of London diners but loyalties can change, especially when an established formula is turned on its head and replaced by something completely new and different. Fortunately, Kettner's had the foresight to plan a sympathetic refurbishment of the premises, using the existing layout and style as the building blocks for the re-launch. And, although the menu is unrecognisable from the restaurant's days as a pizzeria, it is still considerate of the purse strings, with a view to opening its doors to as many patrons as possible.

Kettner's is the kind of restaurant where you can get dressed up to the nines for a glass of bubbly in the famous Champagne Bar, or slip into something more comfortable for a bite to eat in The Brasserie. It's an all-encompassing, welcoming environment that just happens to be stunningly designed and furnished inside. It is a true London classic that has reinvented itself to compete in an ever-changing market and the reception has been warm and welcoming. Theatre goers, party goers, newcomers and old timers are all equally dazzled by the splendid interior of this magnificent building and the name continues to live on.

The Langham

1c Portland Place, W1

If you are looking for a combination of location, interior and food as the key ingredients for a meal, then the awe-inspiring dining room of The Landau at The Langham will tick all the boxes.

When it comes to choosing somewhere to rest their weary heads, the good and the glamorous often plump for The Langham. The name itself conjures up images of timeless sophistication and the hotel certainly doesn't disappoint. Its location is spot-on for anyone dropping into the capital for a few days of business, networking, shopping or interviewing. It is central enough to have everything right on your doorstep and yet discreet enough for celebrities to be able to zip in and out without the encumbrance of paparazzi and wide-eyed Oxford Street shoppers pointing, snapping and staring.

As with all classic London hotels, The Langham comes with its own classic London restaurant. These days, it's not enough to pamper your guests to within an inch of utter relaxation. They must have every conceivable amenity available to them under one roof, and that includes fine dining of the highest order. The Landau is the name of the restaurant that does the honours in The Langham and, if you are looking for a combination of location, interior and

food as the key ingredients for a meal, then this awe-inspiring dining room will tick all the boxes. The Landau used to be the hotel's ballroom so the space had a natural affinity to social gatherings, as well as being a spacious, bright and elegant room in which to locate the new restaurant. The interior has been painstakingly re-worked to produce an environment that is both stately in its splendour but embracing and convivial. Wood panelling, brass light fittings and stunning chandeliers all remind you that this is a premier restaurant on the right side of town.

The Landau offers diners the chance to taste a range of dishes by including a number of tasting menus. There is also the opportunity to dine a la carte. The restaurant has earned a reputation for serving fine European inspired food that relies on the best British ingredients. The flair of the chefs is evident in all the dishes, which are full of surprising twists and elegantly executed diversions from classic recipes. The Landau showcases so much of what is great about London cuisine. The diversity of the food and the elegance of the presentation have ensured that its reputation has spread. As with any good hotel restaurant, it's not just the hotel guests who dine there. Non-guests are constantly clamouring for tables in this Fitzrovia eatery in order to experience the quality of the food and the expertise of the chefs, waiting staff and sommelier.

The Langham has been open since 1865, dedicating itself to the luxury end of the hospitality market and standards haven't slipped an inch since then. The hotel has seen many changes over the years but it remains one of the best addresses in London and a table at The Landau is a coveted booking that will be looked forward to, enjoyed and remembered for a long time afterwards.

Maison Bertaux

28 Greek Street, W1

This dinky restaurant might be light on hearty dishes but it makes its customers want to luxuriate in the simple delight of a pot of tea and a chocolate eclair.

This little French pâtisserie is small on square footage but its reputation is huge. It sells wonderful pastries in the true French tradition and it has been drawing in an appreciative, sweet-toothed clientele since 1871. Londoners have always craved a sugar hit with their morning coffee or afternoon tea and Maison Bertaux has lovingly obliged with an array of gooey delights and sweet treats that have passers-by stopping in their tracks to drool over the window display.

The premises itself is tightly packed onto two floors with a collection of wobbly tables and chairs that give the café the feel of a delightfully antiquated tea room in the heart of the busy city. This is undoubtedly the unique charm of this delightful little hideaway. It is so individual and bursting with character that the whole ceremony of taking tea, or stopping for a bite to eat is reborn. With the glut of chain cafes bombarding every high street and side street, it is so refreshing to be able to indulge a cake craving in an independent establishment that oozes charm and stakes its claim to this patch of Soho turf like a spirited guard dog. Instead of swiping factory-produced muffins from sterile looking counters then

queuing up for conveyor-belt coffee, it feels strangely decadent and indulgent to choose a freshly baked pastry or savoury slice from the tempting display at Maison Bertaux. When such love and attention has gone into the creation of the food, it seems only right that the same care should be given to choosing and eating the cakes. Coffee tends to be slurped from a paper cup whilst dodging human and car traffic on the way to work but Maison Bertaux strives to redress the balance and encourages its customers to linger and savour their food and drinks. After all, a nice cup of tea or coffee provides the opportunity to relax, gather your thoughts and brace yourself for the rest of the day. It is the chance to take time out from the rest of the world, unwind and immerse yourself in your own thoughts or to have a civilised conversation with another human being. And if Maison Bertaux is anything at all, it is civilised.

This dinky restaurant might be light on hearty dishes but it makes its customers want to luxuriate in the simple delight of a pot of tea and a chocolate eclair. Browsing and slowly savouring are positively encouraged and the time-honoured tradition of the lengthy tea or coffee break are held in great esteem here. In the warmer summer months, there's the opportunity to fold yourself into one of the slim tables outside the shop, where you can immerse yourself in the daily to and fro of Soho as you enjoy a light lunch. Upstairs, you can hide yourself away in a corner and pretend the outside world doesn't exist. That's the beauty of Maison Bertaux; it fits your mood. It is a small but perfectly formed homage to the art of simple pleasures.

Patisserie Valerie

44 Old Compton Street, W1

Taking tea in Patisserie Valerie is a well-earned treat and the whole experience is a cut above most other cafes.

Madame Valerie firmly believed that the English needed to be introduced to the delights of traditional continental cakes. So strong were her convictions that she moved to London and opened a patisserie in Soho. A woman's intuition is rarely wrong and the point was proven here as Madame Valerie's shop was a huge success and the pastries were barely out of the oven before eager punters came in to buy them. Little has changed today as our obsession with beautiful sweet treats continues and it is still difficult to pass by this famous shop front without ducking inside for a decadent cake.

Although the premises are still in Soho, the Old Compton Street shop is not the original Patisserie Valerie. This was on Frith Street but, like so many other buildings in London, it was bombed during the war and had to close. However, this didn't put a dampener on Valerie's cake baking mission and she soon set up another shop just a short walk away – the shop that is still open for business today.

Although the glamour and novelty of a French patisserie could well explain the runaway success of the first shop, Patisserie Valerie needed to offer so much more in later years, when cafes and cake shops were springing up all over town. What Patisserie Valerie offered – and indeed still offers – over and above its competitors was a total dedication to produce quality food. The sheer effort that has obviously gone into the creation of the cakes and pastries is astounding and the counter is a feast for all the senses. Taking tea in Patisserie Valerie is a well-earned treat and the whole

experience is a cut above most other cafes.

This focus on excellence was popular with serious cake connoisseurs and it eventually became apparent that one shop just wasn't going to be sufficient to satisfy the cravings of cake crazed Londoners. There are now Patisserie Valerie shops all over London and they have all proved to be just as popular as the original. Every detail is so well judged and everything from a simple almond croissant to a bespoke celebration cake is made with love and care.

Patisserie Valerie is technically now a chain of cafes but each venue has its own unique style and character. Although there is an overriding theme, there is a distinct absence of the corporate monotony and bland branding which denotes so many coffee shops and sandwich bars in the capital. There is a real sense of indulgence here, as if each bite of your Croque Monsieur or Frangipane should be relished and not devoured in a couple of hungry bites between work meetings. This is an opportunity to indulge your taste buds rather than simply satiate and, for true craftsmanship to be appreciated, the food should be enjoyed by the eyes, the mouth and the stomach.

PICCADILLY

Piccadilly is one of the major roads in central London and it is also an area of great historical and commercial importance. With famous names such as the Royal Academy, The Ritz and Fortnum and Mason taking pride of place along the route from Hyde Park Corner to the brash but iconic Piccadilly Circus, there is evidence galore of its elevated place in the history of the city. The cuisine of the area reflects its noble past and a number of well-established and traditional eateries have been satiating the hunger of Londoners for hundreds of years. With the recent revival of classic British cuisine many restaurants have seen their regular customers joined by a new generation of appreciative diners, who are keen to sample the efforts of the best chefs cooking with the best ingredients.

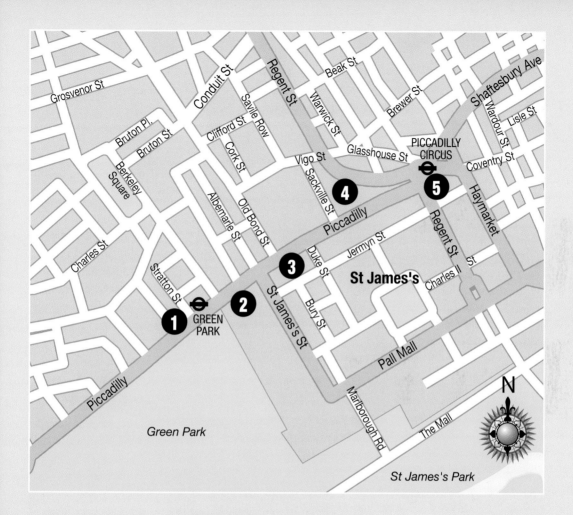

1. Langan's Brasserie
2. The Ritz
3. Fortnum & Mason
4. Bentley's Oyster Bar & Grill
5. Criterion

Bentley's Oyster Bar & Grill

11-15 Swallow Street, W1

Ostensibly an oyster bar, Bentley's is actually so much more.

Although it is situated in the heart of London's bustling West End, you need to either be a regular customer or have a keen sense of direction to locate this famous fish restaurant. Tucked away down a side street between Piccadilly and Regent Street, Bentley's can claim the rare accolade of being in business in the same premises since 1916. You know that a restaurant must be doing something right in order to please its patrons for over 90 years.

When it first opened, the opulent, almost theatrical interior and façade cleverly mimicked the fashion and tastes of the time. It soon became a destination restaurant for the 'it' crowd who lapped up the relaxed atmosphere and decadent seafood morsels on offer in the downstairs bar. Interestingly, despite numerous makeovers and updates over the years, the original layout was similar to how it is today. Whilst theatregoers, socialites and after-work drinkers mingled, sipped and snacked at ground level, the more serious gastronomes were ushered upstairs to the formal dining room. The star ingredient was supplied by the Bentley family's own oyster beds in

Essex. The opening of the restaurant coincided with an increase in popularity and a culinary elevation of this previously humble poor man's staple food.

As the years progressed, Bentley's went from strength to strength, earning critical acclaim from all the influential publications and reviewers of the time. By keeping things simple and allowing the ingredients to speak for themselves, the proprietors built their reputation on the quality of the food that they served. The restaurant was regularly awarded top ratings in guidebooks and it continued to gain a loyal customer base that returned again and again. More recently, Bentley's has undergone a subtle yet dramatic makeover. Having worked as Head Chef at the restaurant, Richard Corrigan bought Bentley's in 2005 and has built on its existing reputation by concentrating on the original no-frills formula. The Michelin-starred chef has worked at some of London's finest establishments but it is his dedication to locally sourced produce and sustainable fish and seafood that has allowed him to carve out his niche at Bentley's. His own culinary values are so intrinsically linked to those of the restaurant's founders that it is no great surprise that Bentley's continues to flourish under his proprietorship. The sympathetic updating of the interior ensured that the original design features remained prominent, with the era being celebrated rather than hidden from view or obliterated by a modern façade.

Ostensibly a Champagne and oyster bar, Bentley's is actually so much more. The cleverly thought-out configuration of the restaurant means that an oyster craving can be swiftly satiated in the ground floor bar, which has a laid-back feel and is set up for casual drinks and dining. A more formal arrangement in the upstairs Grill allows patrons to enjoy the full spectrum of fresh fish and seafood. With Richard Corrigan at the helm, this much-loved London establishment will continue to serve top-quality seafood to a discerning clientele for many years to come.

Criterion

224 Piccadilly, W1

Criterion is a real piece of history in the heart of the West End and you would be hard pressed to find anywhere that equals the remarkable interior and the sense of grandeur that permeates the entire building.

It is said that Arthur Conan Doyle was sitting in the Long Bar in Criterion when he conjured up the initial meeting between his characters Sherlock Holmes and Doctor Watson. So, this illustrious setting has had an important part to play in one of the greatest publishing sensations in the world. But that's not the only momentous occasion in Criterion's history. Since it first opened back in 1874, this extravagant neo-Byzantine design classic has played host to all manner of politicians, pioneers and glitterati. Its location alone warranted its eclectic clientele but it was the opulent interior that kept them coming back. With crushed red velvet chairs, incredibly high, ornately decorated ceilings and gold and marble coming to greet you around every corner, it's easy to see why clandestine meetings were conducted here, deals were done and important political decisions were made.

The Criterion has always specialised in serving an elevated version of good, old-fashioned comfort

Street and yet, despite its stunning façade, it could easily be missed if a shop window was demanding your attention on the other side of the road as you walked by. By blending innocuously into the row of neighbours that share this stretch of Piccadilly, it hides its secret well and the curious, or those in the know, are richly rewarded.

Having recently been taken over by a new owner, the interior has been given a substantial makeover and much of the original glitz and glamour has been injected back into the building. It has a fresh feel to it but one that harks back to the Victorian era: it is as if the essence of Criterion had been captured in a glass phial, hidden for years and is now

food. It is the food we'd like to cook at home if only we had the time, talent and inclination: big, juicy steaks, fresh, delectable seafood and rich, creamy desserts. Of course, it is all done on a far grander scale that one could ever hope to achieve in a domestic environment but then that's the wonderful thing about this restaurant. The heady mix of memory-laden food combined with the utter grandeur of the dining room and the rest of the building creates a surprisingly relaxed yet pampered atmosphere in which to enjoy a meal.

Criterion is a towering haven that protects its visitors from the madness of Piccadilly and Regent

finally being dusted off and allowed out in public once more. With so many pretenders throwing money at lesser establishments, it is refreshing to see a genuinely special piece of dining history being given a new lease of life and the chance to attract a whole new legion of fans.

Criterion is a real piece of history in the heart of the West End and you would be hard pressed to find anywhere that equals the remarkable interior and the sense of grandour that permeates the entire building. It is a deserved entry in London's hallowed club of truly classic restaurants and it has worked hard to earn its place.

Fortnum & Mason

181 Piccadilly, W1

St James's Restaurant at Fortnum's prides itself on having created a menu that relies on seasonal British ingredients, thus reiterating its heritage and the focus on quality, fresh produce.

Fortnum and Mason is quite possibly the most famous and luxurious grocery shop in the world. Founded back in 1707 by William Fortnum and Hugh Mason, it has been supplying British high society with their jam and tea bags ever since. These days, Fortnum and Mason (or Fortnum's as it is fondly called) is so much more than a convenience store. It is a large department store that also includes a hair and beauty salon. For anyone with a phobia of supermarkets, this is definitely the way to shop.

Having been granted a number of Royal Warrants over the years, the Fortnum name is inherently linked to the Royal Family. This has had obvious advantages in terms of the tourist market and the distinctive turquoise and gold packaging makes its way into the suitcases of many people holidaying in London. However, it is not just the Royal connection that has been key to the incredible longevity of this shop.

Fortnum's prides itself on the quality of its produce, the innovations of its products and the loyalty of its staff and customers. A shopping experience at Fortnum's is about so much more than dashing around piling food into a trolley. It is about perusing products and carefully considering the options available; it's about believing in quality, not quantity; and it's about really engaging with the whole shopping experience and using all the senses. And, when you've finished shopping, the stunning St James's restaurant is an oasis in which you can relax, take the weight off your feet and indulge

in a sumptuous feast of top-end food. Although there are a number of restaurants and cafes in Fortnum's, St James's is the best known. It has a reputation for quality fine dining in elegant surroundings and it is open daily for lunch, although lunch is probably not a grand enough word to describe the incredibly diverse and expansive menu on offer. The restaurant prides itself on having created a menu that relies on seasonal British ingredients, thus reiterating its heritage and the focus on quality, fresh produce.

St James's Restaurant is also where you'll find yourself if you choose to indulge in the famous Fortnum's afternoon tea. This much-loved British tradition is the indulgent version of a nice cup of tea

and a biscuit and a number of classic restaurants serve afternoon tea. Fortnum's offers a selection of finger sandwiches, cakes and scones, as well as a huge choice of blended or single estate teas. The St James's afternoon tea tends to be the choice of the tea connoisseur – after all, Fortnum's is well-known for the extensive range of loose leaf teas that it stocks.

Despite its fastidious attention to detail and its classy clientele, Fortnum's remains rooted in its provision of basic, as well as, luxury foodstuffs. If anyone should doubt this, they might like to consider that a forward-thinking Fortnum's was the first shop in Britain to sell Heinz Baked Beans, back in 1886.

Langan's Brasserie
Stratton Street, W1

Langan's has helped to keep British bistro classics at the forefront of the restaurant experience and it champions many of these on its menu.

When the key players of the swinging sixties and seventies were looking for somewhere to eat they had exacting demands. They wanted good food and an atmosphere to match, they didn't necessarily want to get dressed up in suits and ties to go out for a meal, and they certainly didn't want the staid, serious environment and hushed tones that were prevalent in many restaurants at the time. The answer lay in Langan's Brasserie and they flocked there and let the good times roll for many years. It was the popular haunt of singers, artists and other creative types who enjoyed the buzz and the laid-back atmosphere in this central London locale.

In many ways, little has changed since then and Langan's is still cooking good, honest brasserie classics in its kitchen. This is fuss-free, frill-free food that is appreciated as such and the restaurant has been happily going about its business in an

understated way since it first opened. What makes it particularly special is that it was something of a trailblazer all those years ago. It entertained some of the most important British artists of the time, including Francis Bacon and Lucien Freud. In fact, they were so smitten with Langan's and so keen to spend time there, that a number of artists donated paintings in exchange for meals. So, Langan's was not only a restaurant but it was also an art gallery, with these paintings proudly displayed on its cluttered walls.

Today, the restaurant still attracts the old-school patrons who reminisce about the heady days of yesteryear but it also has a new fan base. A simple supper of fish and chips takes on a whole new, glamorous meaning when it is eaten in the auspicious surroundings of the brasserie. The place is teeming with years of accumulated glamour and creativity and it manages to create just the right environment of relaxation and quality

dining. Langan's has helped to keep British bistro classics at the forefront of the restaurant experience and it champions many of these on its menu. Langan's Bangers and Mash with White Onion Sauce is one such example of the legendary dishes that have kept people coming through the doors over the years.

There is no snobbery in the Anglo-French menu and everything is pared down and simply prepared, cooked and presented. There is nothing that will catch out or confuse an unsuspecting diner and when you order, you know exactly what is going to arrive on the plate. Diners are delighted by this simple honesty because the opportunity for disappointment is taken away with the menu. Concisely described dishes, using classic ingredient combinations that everyone knows and loves. That's the Langan's unique selling point and you'd be mad to change a winning formula.

The Ritz

150 Piccadilly, W1

Simply arriving at this fabulous hotel is like walking onto a film set and there is a wonderful sense of occasion that accompanies a meal here.

The Ritz is without a doubt one of the most iconic hotels in London. It was the height of high society sophistication when it first opened its doors in 1906 and little has changed since then with regards to its reputation. The mere mention of the name conjures up images of glamour and indulgence and the hotel certainly does its best to accommodate.

When you step inside The Ritz, you enter another world; a world of carefully judged decadence and over-indulgence which has the sole purpose of pampering its guests and catering to their every whim and requirement. The employees at this illustrious establishment are well used to the expectations of well-heeled, seasoned travellers and their comfort is the main concern here. Guests are cocooned in a gilt-edged world of romance and chivalry, with more swags, tails and ruches than you can shake a stick at. The Ritz restaurant is a magical enclave of otherworldly opulence, all lit up by the sparkly lights of numerous chandeliers – so heavy that the ceiling had to be reinforced to bear their weight.

The site of the Ritz was home to a succession of hotels in its previous life and it is easy to see why. With its prime position on Piccadilly, overlooking Green Park, it was a natural choice for a central London base that also enjoyed a peaceful park vista. When César Ritz acquired the site, he wasted no time in hiring the best architects and designers of the day to help him realise his vision of a grand London hotel. Construction was fast and efficient but there was no scrimping when it came to the amenities and the décor of the hotel. This was to be a jaw-dropping venue that would stun and delight all those who stayed there, as well as providing them with everything they could possibly need during their visit. A Louis XVI theme was adopted throughout the interior of the hotel and the fluidity of the design ensured that the end result was both tasteful and theatrical.

The Ritz restaurant was just one of the many points of pride for the hotel and the ground floor was designed in such a way that all the main rooms and spaces could be viewed from the Long Gallery. As with all historical venues, The Ritz has had to undergo a major set of refurbishment works to ensure its longevity and to continue to enjoy its elevated status. The original design themes were kept very much at heart and the interior has been restored and improved upon, with the restaurant now being amongst the most lavish in the world.

The food is in keeping with the exacting design standards of the dining room and the menu changes seasonally to reflect readily available ingredients and seasonal specialities. There are nods of appreciation to great British classic dishes but these have been given a wonderfully elegant twist, with plates oozing finesse and utterly deserving of their fine-dining status. Dining at The Ritz involves more than just turning up and ordering a meal. The setting, the service and the incredible food make it a far more memorable occasion than most restaurants could hope to provide for their guests. Simply arriving at this fabulous hotel is like walking onto a film set and there is a wonderful sense of occasion that accompanies a meal here. Traditional dinner dances are still held in the restaurant at the weekends so that guests can enjoy the lavish surroundings of the dining room for even longer, as they dance the night away after their meal.

MAYFAIR, ST JAMES'S AND KNIGHTSBRIDGE

These prestigious postcodes are home to some of the finest dining rooms in the capital. Classic London hotels such as Claridge's and The Dorchester offer superlative levels of comfort and customer service to a well-heeled international clientele and the dining experience is also expected to exceed expectations. As such, these establishments have attracted the cream of the crop when it comes to chefs and they have managed to accrue a respectable number of Michelin stars. However, it isn't just restaurants attached to hotels that have caught the attention of discerning diners and Michelin inspectors: Le Gavroche has been dishing up exquisite French fare under the watchful eye of Michel Roux Jr for the past 20 years and his father was at the helm before him.

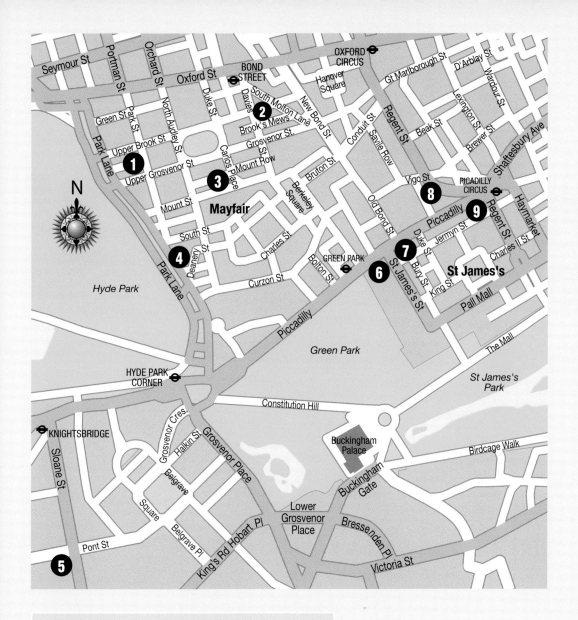

1. Le Gavroche
2. Claridge's
3. Connaught
4. The Dorchester
5. Langtry's
6. The Wolseley
7. Wiltons
8. Veeraswamy
9. Rowley's

Claridge's
Brook Street, W1

Claridge's presents its visitors with a classic British experience and prides itself on the first-class service it offers to guests.

This beautiful hotel pays homage to all things glamorous and opulent. Located in the heart of Mayfair, it has a classic Art Deco inspired design that pays homage to the original building in the 1920s. Although much has been renovated and redesigned in the intervening years, this central theme remains a constant inspiration and many of the original features are still present in the hotel.

With regards to the restaurant, this has undergone a number of transformations and updates and the remnants of some of these early re-designs can still be viewed today. The engraved glass screens of lauded Art Deco designer Basil Ionides remain in the grand space and are a testament to the lasting brilliance of this particular style. More recently, the restaurant has undergone a radical re-design at the hands of New York architect Thierry Despont who has created a lavish room that manages to incorporate contemporary style whilst taking note of its past. There are huge chandeliers and rich, warm fabrics that help to create a more relaxed and cosy dining experience.

The restaurant at Claridge's is a destination for discerning food lovers and it has a deserving reputation as one of the top restaurants in London. Although it has always been renowned for its quality, the ante was upped significantly in 2001 when Michelin-starred chef Gordon Ramsay took over. The chef gave his name to the restaurant and two years later, Gordon Ramsay at Claridge's won a Michelin Star. It is one thing getting a Michelin Star but it's quite something else to hang onto it year after year. Now Chef Patron of the restaurant, Ramsay divides his time between this and his many other establishments and leaves the day-to-day cooking in the capable hands of his Head Chef.

With such a large restaurant operation to contend with, consistency and quality with every plate of food is difficult to achieve. However, as with all other aspects of this grand hotel, everything runs like clockwork and the seamless interaction of the attentive staff ensures that the diners are served swiftly and charmingly. The food that is cooked in the restaurant is based upon the classic techniques that have stood the test of time. The resulting fare is a selection of modern European dishes that highlight the skills of the chefs and the imagination of the Chef Patron. The combination of flavour, presentation and innovation have ensured that tables at Claridge's are booked up many months in advance and are likely to be for the foreseeable future.

Claridge's presents its visitors with a classic British experience and prides itself on the first-class service it offers to guests. The restaurant is no exception and the opulence of the interior is more than matched by the quality of the food and service.

Connaught

Carlos Place, W1

The Connaught has a historical resonance and yet it has also moved fluidly with the times and it continues to immerse itself in contemporary life and culture.

The Connaught is one of London's finest old-school hotels so it makes sense that the restaurant strives for, and lives up to, the same reputation. The five-star hotel recently underwent a huge refurbishment programme and the restaurant was included in this. It coincided with the launch of Hélène Darroze at the Connaught and involved Parisian designer India Mahdavi adding a contemporary elegance to the restaurant without distracting from its sense of history and its location.

Hélène Darroze was already much fêted in her home country of France before bringing her unique take on south-west regional French cuisine to London. Her Parisian restaurant had won two Michelin Stars and, not long after taking the helm at the Connaught, this too caught the eye of the inspectors and was awarded its first Michelin Star. Still, a restaurant shouldn't just be judged on its accolades: a classic restaurant has to combine great food with attentive service, a welcoming atmosphere and a dash of the quirky or unique. The Connaught certainly ticks all the boxes and its impeccable interior and high design standards instantly place it head and shoulders above a great number of its competitors.

As with many top-end restaurants, the Connaught dining room has taken on the personality of the chef. Darroze follows in a line of celebrated and respected chefs working at the peak of their careers, having cooked their way up the culinary ladder. This level of commitment and talent is often rewarded by their name above the entrance door. Prior to Darroze, the hugely skilful Angela Hartnett was in charge. She had worked under Gordon Ramsay for years and has since gone on to work as Chef Patron at Murano, also in Mayfair.

To say that the Connaught has played host to a number of different cuisines over the years is an understatement and yet this has done nothing to detract from its popularity and the high esteem by which it is held by patrons and reviewers alike. Each successive chef has been given carte blanche with the menu and the style of food. They have been allowed the freedom to carve out their own niche whilst staying true to the core principals of a top quality dining experience in the heart of London. So, while Hartnett produced Italian fare, Hélène Darroze is now championing the ingredients and cooking techniques of her native Landes in France.

It is a huge complement to both the chef and the reputation of the restaurant and hotel that this change of direction has had no apparent bearing on its popularity. It proves that excellent food speaks for itself and a metropolitan city like London will always embrace new cooking talent, new flavours and new experiences. The Connaught has a historical resonance and yet it has also moved fluidly with the times and it continues to immerse itself in contemporary life and culture. All these elements combine to make it a classic establishment that is an elegant addition to the Mayfair landscape.

The Dorchester

Park Lane, W1

The Dorchester Grill has always been an integral part of the hotel, serving top-quality British classics to a discerning clientele.

The Dorchester has always been synonymous with traditional British style and luxury. The hotel itself is a popular choice with well-heeled locals looking for an upmarket sleepover venue after a party, as well as tourists eager to sample the best that London has to offer. The service is exceptional: one would expect nothing less in a highly rated establishment. The food served in its restaurants has helped to maintain the hotel's position on the top of the ladder.

As with many other luxury, traditional hotels in London, The Dorchester has an interesting history. When it opened to paying guests in 1931, the building was considered to be quite revolutionary and modern for the time. The site was previously occupied by Dorchester House but the new owners wasted no time in removing all traces of this nineteenth century building in order to make way for the stunning new hotel. The design statements of The Dorchester included large, open-plan spaces that created a light and airy interior that impressed the high society guests. By using reinforced concrete there was no need for supporting pillars. As well as providing an incredible ballroom for guests and visitors, The Dorchester was believed to be the safest hotel in London during the war. As such, it played host to a number of important politicians and dignitaries, all taking refuge in the grandest concrete bunker in town.

The Dorchester Grill has always been an integral part of the hotel, serving top-quality British classics to a discerning clientele. As the years progressed,

the restaurant went from strength to strength, its reputation ensuring that it wasn't just guests of The Dorchester who were lining up to dine in The Grill. A large part of the hotel underwent a significant refit in 1988 and The Grill was extensively overhauled to bring it into line with ultra-modern restaurant service and technology, as well as giving the interior décor a full facelift. The results have been widely acclaimed and this destination restaurant continues to draw in the diners in their droves.

The menu in The Grill is essentially classic British, with signature dishes such as Grilled Dover Sole proving their worth through the generations. It is this consistent nod to classic cooking that has gained The Grill a loyal legion of devotees who wouldn't dream of dining anywhere else whilst in London.

However, the beauty of the restaurant is that is has managed to diversify and experiment within the confines of classic British cuisine. Whilst some dishes have been left untouched, others have been gently and superbly modernised. Head Chefs have respected the timeless classics whilst also adding their personal stamp to the menu. There is an emphasis on fresh, organic produce for maximum flavour and quality.

The Grill at the Dorchester is an undisputed classic restaurant that has fed and watered businessmen, politicians, actors and writers for many years. The food is top-end yet comforting, familiar yet surprising and, above all, memorable. The proof is in the pudding, as they say, and guests seem to return here again and again.

Langtry's
21 Pont Street, SW1

Stepping inside Langtry's is like taking a step back inside a high-society Edwardian dining room.

In many ways Langtry's is the ultimate classic London restaurant. It has so many of the prerequisites that it earns its place on the podium in spades. Firstly, there is the historical aspect of Langtry's, which is a heady cocktail of longevity and celebrity associations. The restaurant used to form part of the house of a famous actress and socialite called Lillie Langtry. She was the toast of Victorian and Edwardian London and also the subject of gossip and scandal when she became Prince Albert's mistress. There's something inherently intriguing about dining in a building that is steeped in history and this stunning setting has been suitably fitted out in a style that befits its grandeur.

However, historical interest pales into insignificance if the food served in a restaurant doesn't live up to a diner's expectations. In Langtry's, the food is a fine complement to the elegant surroundings and the

chef has created a time-honoured homage to British cuisine. The menu reflects the best that British food and ingredients have to offer and classic dishes have been coaxed into the twenty-first century with real flair and a genuine skill and knowledge. Many traditional London dining rooms offer classic dishes but few give them the unusual twists and contemporary styling that are on offer in Langtry's. A simple prawn cocktail is stripped away to its basic elements and then completely re-worked into a culinary classic with stylish execution. The food here is a revelation for anyone keen to sample British food in its modern incarnation.

Forming part of The Cadogan hotel, Langtry's naturally emulates the style and pedigree of this intimate Knightsbridge establishment. However, despite being intrinsically linked, the hotel and restaurant maintain their own distinct characteristics and work independently of each other, as well as complementing one another. The charming style and gorgeous interior of The Cadogan has been extended to the hotel. The two establishment are also linked by their associations with the celebrities of their era. Whilst Lillie Langtry enjoyed the residence of her Knightsbridge home, Oscar Wilde patiently waited for the police to arrive and serve him with a warrant for his arrest in The Cadogan. With such links to the literary and thespian worlds, it is no great surprise that there is an artistic flair that hovers inside both the hotel and restaurant.

Stepping inside Langtry's is like taking a step back inside a high-society Edwardian dining room. The décor is a statement and there are large key pieces that exude grandeur but never detract from the building itself. Modern flourishes are in keeping with the overall style and the interior seems to aptly reflect the food: a contemporary take on much-loved recipes and flavour combinations.

Le Gavroche

43 Upper Brook Street, W1

The Roux brothers, and subsequently, Michel Roux Jr. have worked hard to achieve the incredible reputation that Le Gavroche enjoys.

Le Gavroche has been serving authentic French cuisine of the highest quality since 1967. Back then, the restaurant was located in Lower Sloane Street and it was the culmination of the hard work, drive and passion of the now-famous Roux Brothers, Albert and Michel. Having scrimped, saved, begged and borrowed, they finally realised their dream of opening their own restaurant. It instantly received a hail of rowdy acclaim from the quality-deprived food lovers of the sixties and seventies. Having put up with sub-standard or lacklustre fare for so long, this new French enterprise was like a breath of fresh air on the London culinary scene.

The restaurant moved to its current location in 1981 and just a year later, it was awarded its third Michelin Star, making it the first restaurant in the country to have the coveted three stars. Authenticity and a fastidious attention to detail have ensured that Le Gavroche has remained at the top of its game throughout its history. The restaurant can truly claim to be a family affair as Michel Roux Jr. took over as Chef de Cuisine in 1991. He was determined to stay true to the founding principles of his father's restaurant whilst adding his own distinctive mark to the menu. The plaudits have unanimously agreed that he has achieved his goal and Le Gavroche has earned numerous awards and accolades over the years.

The philosophy is simple: the best of French cuisine with just sufficient twists and flourishes to ensure the menu is exciting, bold and unique. Although Michel Roux Jr. is an innovative chef, he is also mindful of the fact that classic French cookery must underline everything that leaves the kitchen in the restaurant. Such culinary excellence certainly doesn't come cheap and, for most people, dining at Le Gavroche is a once-in-a-lifetime meal. However, by opening for lunch and including a set meal option, Michel Roux Jr. has ensured that the restaurant is accessible to as many people as possible – no mean feat for food cooked at this level.

The name implies a humble background and it means 'urchin', alluding to a character from Les Miserables. It is a wonderful paradox when one considers the status of the food and the restaurant and yet it is strangely fitting. The Roux brothers, and subsequently, Michel Roux Jr. have worked hard to achieve the incredible reputation that Le Gavroche enjoys. They understood perfectly the essential elements of a fine restaurant and they never let them slip. There are exacting standards of service and the same applies to the food. Take your eye off the ball for one minute and there is bound to be a restaurant critic dining in the restaurant that night. It is this consistent attention to every detail that has ensured Le Gavroche is always at the top of the London restaurant pile.

Rowley's

113 Jermyn Street, SW1

Rowley's has kept things simple and traditional when it comes to the menu and this has proven to be a winning formula with its clientele.

Although Rowley's has only been open for business since 1977, it is certainly a true classic on the London restaurant scene. In a previous incarnation, the restaurant site was the home and business premises of the founder of Walls. Now a household name in the meat industry, it began as a fairly humble enterprise, set up by Richard Walls who was an apprentice butcher in St James's Market. Through hard work and expertise he built up an estimable list of customers and the business was passed down through the generations.

Rowley's certainly has echoes of this history, both in the building and in the menu. The dining room includes many classic touches such as starched white tablecloths, wooden floors and elegantly simple dining furniture. Then there are the traditional features that display the links that the restaurant has maintained with the building's past. The ornate ceiling, the antique furnishings and the muted colour palette all help to create an atmosphere of yesteryear within a contemporary context. It is a comfortable space in which to enjoy a meal in this

ancient and historically rich corner of London.

Rowley's has kept things simple and traditional when it comes to the menu and this has proven to be a winning formula with its clientele. British ingredients and dishes are given pride of place and little is done to dilute or disguise the inherent flavours of these quality raw ingredients. It is classic British cuisine executed with great confidence. The speciality is char-grilled entrecote steak with the famous Rowley's herb and butter sauce. This is served with an unlimited supply of French fries or chunky chips and this small detail is very telling about the entire Rowley's enterprise. Whilst the highest standards of food and service are consistently maintained, there is also a very relaxed and informal air about the place. Great importance is placed on the enjoyment of the food. The continued appearance of classic dishes shows the level of regard and loyalty that regular patrons have

for the restaurant, and indeed, the appreciation that Rowley's has for them.

When a restaurant becomes well known for certain dishes that appear on its menu then it has almost certainly made it into the echelon of classic restaurant territory. It is high praise indeed for a specific dish to be singled out and then sought out by other people looking to recreate a dining experience as recommended by a friend or colleague. This is how reputations are built and it is certainly the way in which a particular establishment builds up a loyal customer base. Humans are essentially creatures of habit who will gladly re-order a particularly memorable meal in a particularly memorable restaurant again and again. Rowley's is a luxurious comfort zone serving luxurious comfort food. It is hardly surprising that so many people have fallen for its charms over the years.

Veeraswamy

Victory House, 99 Regent Street, W1

Veeraswamy demonstrates the rich diversity of Indian cuisine and it continues to experiment with cutting-edge ideas that elevate it beyond most of its competitors.

Veeraswamy is the oldest Indian restaurant in London and also one of the finest. With its lofty location, perched above the hectic grandeur of Regent Street, it has everything going for it and yet it ensures the food served in the luxurious dining room is always the star of the show.

The restaurant was first opened in 1926, in the same premises it occupies today. The year heralded the beginning of the Art Deco movement and also a bit of an awakening of the population's taste buds. Although eating out was still a rare treat for most people, fine dining was becoming more common and the roaring twenties ensured that social interaction was moved up the agenda and people were beginning to have a greater choice as far as restaurants were concerned.

The original owners of Veeraswamy would have certainly been a big draw. The wonderful

combination of the great grandson of an English General, and an Indian princess gave the restaurant gravitas and authenticity right from the start. It proved popular with British military personnel keen to re-live some of the culinary experiences they had enjoyed on their tours of duty in India. However, the cuisine gradually became more popular with a wider audience and the British began to fall in love with the heady aromas and pungent flavourings of this exotic food. Having spent so long trying to get creative with ration books and paltry selections of meat and vegetables, the weary taste buds of Londoners were given a new lease of life.

Today, the restaurant is as popular as ever and the menu spans every corner of the Indian sub-continent, allowing diners to sample dishes from across this vast and culinary diverse country. Classic dishes have been included but there are also plenty of examples of contemporary Indian cuisine: recipes that have been created by the new wave of talented young chefs keen to experiment with the use of spicing in food. Veeraswamy is geared towards providing diners with a unique insight into the complexities and subtleties of Indian cuisine and this is done skilfully and artistically.

Whilst the food is of the highest quality, the interior can't fail to impress diners either. The restaurant has recently been refurbished and it embraces the opulence of 1920s India, with the great palaces of the Maharajas as its influence. There is lavish carpeting and seating, as well as a wonderful array of brightly coloured lights and a decadent chandelier. This new interior certainly helps to set the scene for the meal ahead and diners are fully aware that they are about to indulge in a rare culinary treat.

It is a testament to the skills of the chefs that Veeraswamy has managed not only to survive, but also to thrive, in its central London location for such a long time. Having set the scene for exclusive

Indian dining, it inadvertently filled a gap in the market when diners went looking for a curry restaurant that could supply something more than a pint and a chicken tikka masala after the pub on a Friday night. Veeraswamy demonstrates the rich diversity of Indian cuisine and it continues to experiment with cutting-edge ideas that elevate it beyond most of its competitors.

Wiltons

55 Jermyn Street, SW1

Wiltons has secured itself a firmly established place in the hearts of traditional food lovers in London.

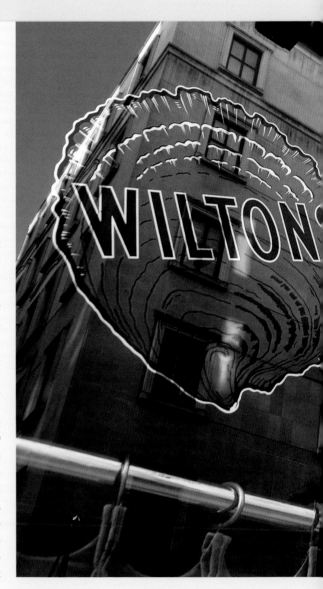

As classic London restaurants go, you would be hard-pressed to find an establishment more deserving of the accolade than Wiltons. It has been serving its brand of traditional British cuisine for well over 150 years and it specialises in seafood and game, prepared and cooked in classic ways.

Although Wiltons didn't become an established restaurant until 1840, the name and the business had been in existence since 1742 when George William Wilton sold shellfish from a stall in Haymarket. As the business expanded so did the premises and eventually George's nephew, William, was in charge of Wiltons Shellfish Mongers and Oyster Rooms, in Cockspur Street. The premises never moved very far but the establishment did change location a number of times over the years, each time widening its customer base and expanding on its ever-growing business. The latest move to its current address was in 1984 and the restaurant has been serving politicians, actors and public figures in its immaculate dining room ever since.

The simple, uncluttered menu is a delight to the eyes and it features a minimalist list of carefully selected fish and seafood dishes, as well as items from the grill, and game, when it is in season. This is true British cooking that relies on the seasonality of ingredients, thus offering its patrons the best that the UK has to offer in the seasons that it is available. The classic nature of the thinking behind the dishes and the preparation of the food have ensured that

Wiltons has maintained a quiet but distinctive respectability among its regulars and an appreciation for top-quality British cuisine from those who arrive here to dine for the first time.

The décor has echoes of the stately home about it but not in the stuffy, rarely used sense. It has been put together with a great deal of thought and the coordination of colours, furnishings and adornments testifies to the tasteful exclusivity of this much-loved establishment. It is inviting but maintains an air of formality that puts customers at ease and reassures them of the expertise and knowledge of the staff. Wiltons is used to entertaining high profile customers and has succeeded in creating an environment in which service is paramount and the food is exceptional. The simplicity of most of the dishes serves to highlight the quality of the raw ingredients and the ability of the chefs to stand back and allow this to shine through.

Wiltons has secured itself a firmly established place in the hearts of traditional food lovers in London. It name is synonymous with quality – both of food and service – and it continues to delight its patrons by specialising in British food that many other restaurants have turned away from, in order to concentrate on profits.

CAFÉ~RESTAURANT

The Wolseley

160 Piccadilly, W1

The winning combination of good food, attentive service and stunning interior have propelled The Wolseley to the top of London's restaurant league.

In previous incarnations, the building that houses The Wolseley was a car showroom and a bank. Originally designed by William Curtis Green in 1921, the stunning interior was used to show off the pride of The Wolseley Motors collection. Unfortunately, the cars didn't endear themselves to the general public and the company was forced to sell the premises. It remained a bank until The Wolseley restaurant opened in 2003 to immediate acclaim. Now the haunt of office workers, savvy tourists, media moguls and paparazzi-shy celebrities, The Wolseley is one of the ultimate classic London eateries with achingly cool credentials.

The interior has been lovingly restored to its former glory but the new owners kept elements of its past as well and the whole works wonderfully. There are incredibly high ceilings, lush wood and brass fittings and elaborate metalwork on the staircase. The design has been created to provide big gestures and yet the main dining area is incredibly cosy and welcoming. It is a large, open-plan space that has numerous nooks and crannies and tucked away tables, making it the ideal spot to indulge in a lingering lunch or dinner. Not that that's all you can eat at The Wolseley. It has become a haven for all-day dining, beginning with breakfast and then working its way through lunch, afternoon tea and all the way to dinner. This results in a bustling restaurant that has no stints of gaping emptiness between sittings. There is always something going on and plenty of opportunities for some surrupticious people watching.

The menu is a fresh and light Anglo-French hybrid of brasserie classics and British stalwarts: a bevy of crowd pleasers that ensures there is something for everyone. It is classy gastro-café food served in the grandest of dining rooms by waiting staff who appear to glide around on a wave of efficiency. This winning combination of good food, attentive service and stunning interior have propelled The Wolseley to the top of London's restaurant league and it has secured a worldwide reputation in a relatively short space of time. Its location has obviously had some part to play in its success but this particular establishment has no need to rely on passing trade to fill the tables: it can be booked up for weeks in advance.

The Wolseley offers a great solution to the perennial 'quick bite to eat' question. No matter what time of the day, you can pamper your taste buds in an elegant space without the brisk formality of other restaurants. Dress codes don't apply but the service and food will knock the socks off the competition. So many average establishments serve average bistro food for extortionate prices. It makes a refreshing change to be able to enjoy everything from eggs Benedict to steak frites in such a welcoming and impeccably presented restaurant.

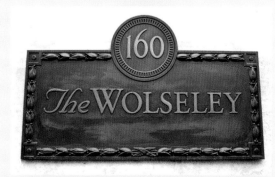

COVENT GARDEN

Covent Garden sits geographically in the heart of London and it is also at the heart of the cultural and dining scene. Although the area is a tourist hub with certain restaurants tripping over themselves to get people through the doors for mediocre meals, there is also a fine selection of eateries with a substantially higher pedigree. Rules has been serving authentic English cuisine for over 200 years, making it the oldest restaurant in the capital, whilst The Ivy shields celebrities from the paparazzi and offers a no-nonsense menu of comforting classics. J. Sheekey is another safe haven for famous faces and is famous itself for the incomparable fish and seafood that comes out of its kitchen. Covent Garden is an epicure's delight with its wealth of quality restaurants offering world-class cuisine.

1. The Rock & Sole Plaice
2. Punjab
3. Mon Plaisir

4. The Ivy
5. J. Sheekey
6. Rules

The Ivy

1-5 West Street, WC2

Dining at The Ivy is like going round to a good friend's house: the service is attentive and personal; the food is unpretentious and guests always leave with a full tummy and a smile on their face.

If you haven't heard of The Ivy then you probably haven't heard of any London restaurants. So renowned is this Covent Garden stalwart that it is still difficult to secure a booking unless you book online for pre- or post-theatre. It also remains one of the dining venues of choice for many well-known personas from all walks of life. Publishers go there to toast book deals, film studio executives go there to sign contracts and pretty much everyone goes there to be seen. It is a restaurant that oozes class and sophistication as well as serving some of the best food in London – why wouldn't you want to be seen there?

The Ivy has been serving sumptuous comfort food in its intimate dining room since 1917. Its Covent Garden position made it an immediate hit with the theatre fraternity – both actors and audience. Word soon got around that this was a cosy haven close to work where egos would be delicately soothed and the famous could dine out in style. The original owner of The Ivy was Abel Giandellini and it was his successful partnership with Mario Gallati that helped to shape the restaurant that stands today. The original ethos was all about providing a welcoming environment for guests and designing a menu that was based around classic dishes.

Although the restaurant has undergone a number of incarnations over the years, more recently the refurbishments have taken the dining room back to something that more closely resembles its original appearance. The distinctive stained glass windows ensure privacy once diners are seated inside and the warm, wood tones make everyone feel instantly at home. To have stood the test of time and still be attracting the London glitterati is no small achievement. Trendy bars and restaurants spring up all over the Capital all the time and people often trip over themselves trying to secure a table and make sure they are seen going in or coming out. However, the pride that The Ivy takes in looking after its regular customers is just one of its well-known attributes. Dining at The Ivy is like going round to a good friend's house: the service is attentive and personal; the food is unpretentious and guests always leave with a full tummy and a smile on their face, promising to come back soon.

Many top-end restaurants strive for innovation and cutting-edge presentation in their food. Although this undoubtedly makes for a stunning meal, it's not the kind of food that people choose to eat every day. The Ivy has carved out its culinary niche by serving food that is everyday exemplary: dishes that evoke memories of childhood; holidays; or family gatherings. So, you'll find things like creamy risotto, succulent roast chicken and shepherd's pie on the menu. But they will be prepared and cooked in such a way that they surpass your memories and really engage your taste buds. People return for the comfort they find in the food and this combination of fine dining and classic dishes is both unusual and admirable. The Ivy has been filling this gap in the market for nearly one hundred years and it shows no sign of slowing down or losing its appeal.

J. Sheekey

28-34 St Martin's Court, WC2

J. Sheekey has perfected the art of turning the humble fish into a meal fit for a King without losing sight of the importance of the main ingredient.

This venerable old restaurant is like a much-respected great uncle. It has occupied its space on St Martin's Court since 1896 and has been serving quality shellfish and fish dishes ever since. J. Sheekey is another comfort food stop on the actors' London restaurant tour. It is located a matter of metres from some of the best-known theatres in the Capital so there is no shortage of theatrical patrons passing through the doors.

The size and grandeur of the current configuration of the restaurant bears little resemblance to the somewhat humbler, original Sheekey. This was a small affair that was located in Lord Salisbury's new St. Martin's Court development. Josef Sheekey was a fishmonger who sold his seafood from a market stall. He was given permission to start serving meals in St. Martin's Court under the proviso that he would prepare food for Lord Salisbury's private guests when they came for dinner after a theatre performance. 'Mighty oaks from little acorns grow', as the saying goes and it wasn't long before Josef's simple seafood suppers were attracting ravenous Londoners from all over the West End. In the following years the restaurant grew, both in reputation and in physical size. It gradually took over buildings on either side to create a larger dining area for its ever-increasing clientele.

This desire to expand has almost taken on a will of its own and it seems that J. Sheekey will never tire of squeezing outwards into its Covent Garden environs. In 2008, yet more space magically appeared in order to create the Oyster Bar. It seems fitting that a fish restaurant with such a first-class reputation should add a specialist room to cater to the insatiable palate of oyster connoisseurs. Here, diners can sit up at the bar and enjoy a variety of fish-based snacks and bites with centre stage obviously being given to the mighty bivalve, not to mention old favourites like the fish pie. This kind of dining has become increasingly popular and J. Sheekey has shown that it is a restaurant that is keen to move with the times, whilst retaining its sense of history and tradition.

The restaurant itself is warm and inviting, fuss-free but at the same time cosy. Crisp, clean linen complements the wood panelled walls and diners are immediately aware of the stature of this hallowed London dining room. It really is a fish-lover's paradise because the menu sings with the sound of the sea and your taste buds are doing somersaults before the food arrives. The expected array of tantalising shellfish will help to whet your appetite and keep hunger at bay and then you can opt for a light, grilled fish dish or indulge yourself with a classic helping of fish pie. J. Sheekey has perfected the art of turning the humble fish into a meal fit for a King. The fish is very much the star of the dish and the cooking techniques and accompaniments are there to enhance the flavour, rather than overpower it.

Long-time patrons of the restaurant were concerned when it hit financial difficulties in the nineties. Much breath was held as negotiations took place about its future. It would have been a travesty to allow this gem to simply fade away but luckily, Caprice Holdings Ltd bought it and brought it back from the brink. It was lovingly restored, re-launched and is once again the place to be seen.

Mon Plaisir

19-21 Monmouth Street, WC2

Mon Plaisir continues to do what it has done best since first opening: providing a warm, Gallic welcome and serving patrons with a selection of classic recipes that form the backbone of French cuisine.

Mon Plaisir claims the crown for being London's oldest French restaurant and it has proven its worth over the years with its staple menu stocked with classic Gallic dishes. Located in the heart of bustling Covent Garden, this little corner of France has proudly served patrons from all over the globe wishing to dine out in style. However, it has also proven to be a welcome retreat for French diners yearning for some of the flavours of home and, as such, the proudest examples of French rustic cooking are prominent here.

The restaurant itself venerates and celebrates all things French. In case there was any confusion about the address, a large Tricolor hangs above the entrance and memorabilia adorns the eclectic interior. In the 65 years since it first opened its doors to the paying public, the somewhat svelte girth of Mon Plaisir has expanded considerably, spilling out into neighbouring rooms. It began as a modest little dining room catering to a handful of homesick French and some adventurous locals but has grown into a four-room restaurant suite that can accommodate 100 hungry customers at any one time. This expansion is down to the hard work and commitment of the Lhermitte family, who have owned the restaurant since 1972 after taking over from the Viala brothers.

The interior is a medley of styles, with each dining room setting the scene of its particular era or influences. So, you could be dining in an art deco-inspired space or a cosy attic that resembles an artisan's cottage. However, for those who have made Mon Plaisir their second home over the years, it has to be a table in 'The Front'. Regulars are greeted like old friends and ushered into their usual seats in the front room as soon as they come through the door. This is the original dining area of the restaurant and little has changed here in the intervening years. The diverse design strategy at Mon Plaisir lends a miscellany to the restaurant that you won't find replicated elsewhere. It's the culmination of years of passion and a genuine belief in the philosophy of the restaurant by the owners. Mon Plaisir holds an important place in London's recent culinary history as it demonstrates the diversity of the population and also their desire to experience new cuisines. Whilst the British are now on familiar terms with dishes like Steak Tartare and Coq au Vin, this would have been cutting edge dining for newcomers to the French table back in the fifties and sixties.

Today, Mon Plaisir continues to do what it has done best since first opening: providing a warm, Gallic welcome and serving patrons with a selection of classic recipes that form the backbone of French cuisine. Whilst flourishes of modernity sprinkle themselves liberally across the menu, at its heart it stays true to its roots and doesn't stray too far from the cooking methods employed by generations of French chefs. It is a proud establishment and with good reason. So much has been achieved here and it remains a stalwart for traditional cooking in a world of modern ideas.

Punjab

80 Neal Street, WC2

This family run establishment has not only carved out a niche for itself with a loyal customer base but it also paved the way for a succession of Indian restaurants.

Today, there is an Indian restaurant on virtually every high street and we are spoilt for choice when it comes to eating one of the nation's favourite foods. Different restaurants specialise in cuisines from different regions and it is possible to sample dishes from all over India without leaving London. However, in 1947, the concept of going out for a curry or ordering an Indian takeaway was virtually unheard of. The war had just ended and eating out at all was considered a luxury. Yet it was against these unfavourable odds that Gurbachan Singh Maan opened Punjab, a restaurant that served dishes from his native North India.

It might sound like a recipe for disaster to open a restaurant during the food rationing years. But more than that, it was a restaurant serving food that most of the population had never even heard of, let alone tried. And yet, it was actually quite a good time to be a pioneer for Indian food. With a growing resident Indian population, including many diplomats and businessmen based in London, Gurbachan Singh Maan spotted a big gap in the market and he took his chance. The restaurant has remained in the family ever since, with Gurbachan's grandson, Sital, buying Punjab from his grandfather in 1971. However, it hasn't always been located in Covent Garden. The original restaurant was in the City of London but the savvy Gurbachan realised the benefits of relocating to the heart of the West End. Here passing trade would be greater and it was a location where people naturally sought out restaurants before and after theatre performances.

The interior of the restaurant is simply and tastefully decorated with muted colours and photographs adorning the walls. The space is deceptively large and the restaurant is usually bustling, with capable waiting staff winding their way around the tables, delivering the freshly prepared dishes to hungry diners.

Punjabi food is fragrant and flavoursome but not as heavily spiced as food from some of the other regions in India. The spices are subtle and the dishes don't have an immediate heat that has customers reaching for their pint glass to try and cool their mouths down. Punjabi cuisine incorporates spices to complement the main ingredient of the dish, rather than to dominate it. Yet the dishes can be extremely complex, with a large number of ingredients being combined to produce pastes and sauces.

Punjab was certainly responsible for helping to introduce a whole generation of Londoners to Indian food. The move to Covent Garden helped the restaurant to appeal to a wider audience but it was the food itself that really put Punjab on London's culinary map. The very nature of good quality, home cooking means it is naturally imbued with the passion and creativity of the chef who prepared it. This family run establishment has carved out a niche for itself with a loyal customer base but it also paved the way for a succession of Indian restaurants and turned Britain into a nation of Indian food lovers.

The Rock & Sole Plaice

47 Endell Street, WC2

Although The Rock & Sole Plaice can't claim to be the oldest fish and chip shop in the capital, it wasn't lagging too far behind the first restaurant and it has survived the longest.

Much is made of the quality of food in London restaurants nowadays, with a new breed of chefs creating adventurous, modern British cuisine that has earned them a worldwide reputation. However, if you were to stop any passer-by on the street and ask them what the national dish of England is, nine times out of ten the answer would be fish and chips.

There has been some discrepancy over where the first portion of fish and chips was sold in the country, with London and Lancashire both claiming to be home to the first restaurant specialising in this comforting delicacy. What is known is that fish and chip shops were opened in both locations in the 1860s and there is now one in pretty much every town, village and hamlet in the country. Potatoes and fish were cheap, staple foods in the nineteenth century and deep-frying them transformed them into a deliciously wholesome, somewhat nutritious and mouth-wateringly enticing meal. A batch of chips and battered fish could be produced quickly and economically and it wasn't long before the population was wholeheartedly embracing this finger-licking meal. Traditionally wrapped in newspaper, the piping hot fish and chips could be eaten on the go, or taken home for a much-anticipated family treat.

Although The Rock & Sole Plaice can't claim to be the oldest fish and chip shop in the capital, it wasn't lagging too far behind the first restaurant and it has survived the longest. Opened in 1871, it has been serving traditional fish and chips to hungry customers ever since. The great thing about this classic combination is that there is little room for

improvement or variation and fish and chips are prepared here in much the same way as they always have been. However, that's not to say that all plates of this British favourite are the same. There are plenty of opportunities to slip up and get it wrong and perhaps the fact that The Rock & Sole Plaice is still eminently popular proves its worth. The batter must be prepared in the correct way, the fat must be the right temperature and the fish must be left to drain for sufficient time. It also goes without saying that the raw ingredients must be of the best quality. When all the rules are followed and fish and chips are prepared with the correct amount of care and attention, it's a meal that will put a smile of satisfaction on your face.

For fish and chip fans this restaurant is well worth travelling to. There is a takeaway counter and some seating upstairs from where you can enjoy the hustle and bustle of a busy service. Alternatively, the staircase leads down to a tiny basement dining room that hums with conversation and the rapid clink of cutlery as hungry diners devour their dinner. The menu is largely a reassuring selection of standard fish and chip fare with a few more adventurous offerings for those who want to branch out of their chip shop comfort zone. And, whilst it is always nice to try something new, it is equally enjoyable to immerse yourself in the familiarity of a tried-and-tested culinary formula. After all, 140 years' worth of diners can't have got it wrong.

Rules

35 Maiden Lane, WC2

Rules specialises in classic British culinary traditions, specifically game, shellfish and pies. The quality of the ingredients that it sources ensures that the food is worthy of the restaurant's worldwide reputation.

As London's oldest restaurant, Rules has a pedigree all of its own. It has played host to Royalty, aristocracy and celebrities by the dozen. It has survived wars, recessions and changing tastes and it remains as popular today as when it first opened in 1798. It seems incredible that a restaurant could have survived for over 200 years in the same building, serving the same style of food but then not every restaurant is Rules. What is perhaps even more incredible is that, in all this time, Rules has only been in the ownership of three families – but perhaps this is simply another of the secrets to its success.

Rules specialises in classic British culinary traditions, specifically game, shellfish and pies. The quality of the ingredients that it sources ensures that the food is worthy of the restaurant's worldwide reputation. This is certainly the place to dine if you are a fan of game and the menu reflects the often underappreciated variety of game on offer in Britain with roe deer, hare and partridge just some of the permanent fixtures on the menu. Other game appears at the onset of the hunting season, with some being subject to availability. This level of uncertainty adds to the kudos of the restaurant because it reassures (if reassurance were needed) that everything is seasonal; the food served being that which is naturally available.

Inside the restaurant, the décor aptly reflects the style of the food and the status of the establishment. Plush furnishings jostle for pride of place, whilst practically every inch of wall space is taken up with an eclectic collection of

paintings and drawings, reflecting the long and illustrious history of the building. A warm, ambient glow gives the dining room a sense of cosy warmth on cold winter evenings, which is exactly the atmosphere that one craves when waiting for a hot, meat and suet pie to arrive at the table. Despite the widespread recognition of Rules, this is not an establishment that trades on the fact that it is the oldest restaurant in London. It is certainly a talking point and a famous name can help to overcome obstacles because nostalgia and history can be so seductive. However, with Rules, this is certainly an aside to the meal itself as standards are never let slip. Indeed, there seems to be even more to live up to in order to ensure that the reputation is continually earned on the merits of the food and not the age of the restaurant.

Rules has remained true to the original concept of the restaurant and its sturdy British menu has more than stood the test of time. As taste buds have swayed precariously from one cuisine to another, Rules has managed to stick to its principles and remain comfortably in the niche that it carved out for itself all those years ago. It continues to provide a traditional dining environment and stalwart British menu in the heart of London.

SOUTH LONDON

South London has traditionally been viewed as the poor relation when it comes to eating out in London. It is true that Michelin stars and celebrity hangouts have tended to congregate in the West End but that doesn't mean taste buds will go unsatisfied south of the river: far from it. The food here is earnest, honest and hard working. The recent pie and mash renaissance is meaningless to South Londoners who have been enjoying this working class staple for the last century. Much-loved establishments such as M. Manze and Arments serve large portions of food with refreshingly unfussy presentation. However, there is also plenty of sophistication down south as well. The stunning location and renowned menu of Beauberry House in Dulwich has helped to propel it to lofty heights.

Tulse Hill

Croxted Rd
Turney Rd

Dulwich

Dulwich Park

Rosendale Rd

College Rd

Rd College

● Beauberry House

Dulwich

Park Rd

Croxted Rd

Rosendale Rd

Alleyn Park Rd

College Rd

Lancaster Ave

Tulsemere Rd

Hunt's Slip Rd

Ardiul Rd

Idmiston Rd

N

Park Rd

Penton Pl

Amelia St

Walworth Rd

Browning St

East St

Walworth

Braganza St

Manor Place

East St

Portland St

Thurlow St

Kinglake St

Penrose St

Liverpool Gr

Merrow

Villa St

Albany Rd

Westcott Rd

Fielding St

● Arments

Lorrimore Rd

Westmoreland Rd

Burgess Park

Cook's Rd

Albany Rd

John Ruskin St

Camberwell Rd

New Church Rd

Wells Way

St Georges

Bethwin Rd

Edmund St

Wyndham Rd

Camberwell

N

Bermondsey St

Tanner

Tooley St

Druid St

Long Lane

Swan St

Tabard St

Great Dover St

Tower Bridge Rd

Abbey St

The Grange

Harper Rd

Falmouth Rd

● M. Manze

Grange Rd

Spa Road

Tower Bridge Rd

New Kent Rd

Searles Rd

Page's Walk

Willow Way

Bermondsey

N

Chatham St

Rodney Rd

Old Kent Rd

Mandela Rd

Dunton Rd

Arments

7&9 Westmoreland Road, SE17

After almost 100 years of serving its famous pie and mash, Arments seems to be growing in popularity and is introducing this classic dish to an ever greater audience.

Arments is a true family establishment, with the business having been passed down the generations since the first portion of pie and mash was sold on the premises in 1914. Nowadays we would shudder at the thought of a fledgling business being opened in the same year that heralded the beginning of World War One. However, the Arments didn't see this as a disadvantage and they have certainly gone on to prove this over the decades.

The menu has changed very little over the years but then Arments is a traditional pie and mash shop and connoisseurs of the cuisine would be up in arms if the original combinations of ingredients on the plate, or the pie fillings, were altered in any way. Pie and mash shops serve pie and mash, in the same way that fish and chip shops serve fish and chips: prepare it well, cook it well but never change the menu. Although pie and mash was the takeout of choice during the beginning of the last century, shops slowly and quietly closed down, leaving just a few stalwarts to serve this classic British fare (also see M. Manze on page 104). However, there has been something of a resurgence in the popularity of traditional British food in the last few years and pie and mash is once again appearing with pride on restaurant menus.

Arments prepare all their pies and their mash on site so everything is cooked on the day that it is served and this marks the establishment out as a purveyor of truly authentic home-cooked food. The restaurant is regularly full to capacity and the rapacious appetite of the British pie fanatic is glaringly obvious from the stacks of empty plates that are collected from the tables. Arments also specialises in that other working class culinary hero – the jellied eel. Once again, these are all prepared on the premises and ordered with gusto by the appreciative diners. Arments must be commended for helping to keep a great British tradition alive, and not only alive but positively thriving. They take huge pride in the food that is prepared here and they have ensured that pie and mash is still readily available for Londoners to take away or to enjoy in the restaurant.

The history of the city is closely intertwined with its restaurants and major events can often be linked to the food that was eaten at the time and the places where people dined. Pie and mash was very much a staple food for working class Londoners and it was the first mainstream takeaway. It represented hearty food that could be produced quickly and cost effectively and the basic principles still apply to much take away food today. However, you would be hard pressed to find a takeaway that matches the quality and consistency of Arments. After almost 100 years of serving its famous pie and mash, the restaurant seems to be growing in popularity and is introducing this classic dish to an ever greater audience.

Beauberry House

Gallery Road, West Dulwich, SE21

The clientele here can enjoy everything from a laid-back weekend brunch to a fine dining experience that challenges the best in terms of the quality of the food, the service and the ambience.

Beauberry House has a long and illustrious history that stretches back to 1785. It was in that year that the original house was built on the grounds of the estate by the owner, John Willies. In the ensuing two hundred-plus years, the house and grounds have undergone a massive transformation and have passed through the ownership of many different people.

The original house was called College Place but in 1818 the new owner, Charles Rankin, changed the name to Belair. Following Rankin, a sheriff, a paper merchant and then the army took up residence in the grand building at different stages in its history. Each tenant changed the character of the property to a greater or lesser degree, as extensions were added, repairs were made and sections of the building were used or allowed to fall into gradual disrepair over the years. Eventually the wear and tear took its toll and, in 1946, Southwark Council took over the lease and began a programme of redevelopment.

It wasn't until 1996 that the grandeur of this imposing building finally came into its own and Belair House was opened to the public as a restaurant and bar. With its beautiful scenic location and impressive façade, it soon became a destination eatery, as much for its ambience as for the quality of its food. In 2004, the most recent proprietor, Ibi Issolah, took over the building. Along with a full-scale refurbishment came another name change and Beauberry House was born. Having already attracted critical acclaim with his central London restaurant, L'Etranger, Issolah developed the dining areas and transformed Beauberry House into a restaurant and venue that caters to every occasion; an essential attribute for an out-of-town venue that relies on word of mouth rather than passing trade. More recently, Beauberry House has earned a deserved reputation as one of the finest wedding venues in the capital. It enjoys unparalleled views over the surrounding parkland and the building itself is truly awe-inspiring, with that all-important photogenic quality.

A number of different menus allude to the versatility of the dining experience at Beauberry House. The clientele can enjoy everything from a laid-back weekend brunch to a fine dining experience that challenges the best in terms of the quality of the food, the service and the ambience. All the food is lovingly created with the same attention to detail, however, the lack of pretension results in a relaxed atmosphere, despite the almost stately environment. This juxtaposition of formal and informal is what makes Beauberry House truly unique amongst London's restaurants. Issolah has succeeded in creating an exclusive eatery that is accessible to everyone. Beauberry House has always had an important role to play in the local community and Dulwich residents are rightly proud of this gem on their doorstep.

M. Manze

87 Tower Bridge Road, SE1

M. Manze is one of the last surviving traditional pie and mash shops in London and it also happens to be the oldest, having been in business since 1902.

Although there are many criteria that lead to a restaurant being regarded as a 'classic', these do not necessarily include its location, the price of its menu, the amount of money that has been spent on its interior or how long in advance you need to book in order to secure a table. M. Manze certainly hasn't splashed the cash in terms of its décor or furnishings. It operates on a first come, first served policy and you can eat until you need to loosen your belt for a handful of loose change. And yet, this proud South-East London establishment is as deserving of its place in the list as any other restaurant.

Pie and mash shops were a common sight across south and east London over the last hundred years. These were largely working class areas and pie and mash, along with the East End

staple – jellied eels – provided a hearty, nutritious meal for very little money. As areas changed and culinary tastes were pulled in various different directions, these basic restaurants, supplying cheap food to the masses, began to lose custom and many of them were forced to close down. M. Manze is one of the last surviving traditional pie and mash shops in London and it also happens to be the oldest, having been in business since 1902.

It was Michele Manze who established the restaurant. His family was originally from Italy but they settled in Bermondsey when Michele was a baby. The family had traditionally been in the ice cream business but Michele spotted a gap in the market for affordable, filling fare and the first M. Manze pie and mash shop was an instant

success. Several other shops followed over the years and the Manze in Peckham still survives, although others were destroyed in the war. The business has remained in the family and a third shop was opened ten years ago in Sutton, proving that there has been something of a revival of late for traditional British working class food.

The retro interior of the restaurant is a no-nonsense set-up that comprises a long counter along one side and simple bench seating along the other. It is as basic and uncluttered as the food that is served inside. The menu doesn't take long to peruse and it really comes down to quantities – you can opt for one or two homemade beef pastry pies and a single or double serving of mash. There is liquor (parsley sauce) and jellied eels for those looking for a truly authentic meal and there's a nod to contemporary tastes with the inclusion of a vegetarian pie. But that's just about it. No side dishes, no choice of vegetables, no garnishes, jus or fancy cooking techniques – what you see is absolutely what you get.

Over the years, M. Manze has played an important role in the community and it is so much more than just a restaurant. It has been a meeting place, providing a particularly welcome retreat for older residents, many of whom have been eating in Manze's since their childhood. It has also given families the opportunity to eat out together. It is a far cry from fine dining but this old-fashioned, honest, comfort food is accessible to everyone and Manze has made it viable for low-income families to enjoy a meal out in a restaurant.

With the opening of the third restaurant in the chain, it seems that the Manze brand of no-frills food has earned a fair number of new fans. It has fed hundreds of thousands of hungry South Londoners over the years and, if the queues outside the Bermondsey restaurant on Saturday lunchtimes are anything to go by, business shows no signs of letting up just yet.

EAST LONDON AND THE CITY

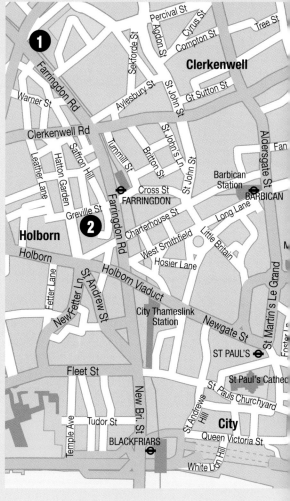

The larger than life East End blends into the fast-paced City of London with a subtle but discernible blurring of boundaries. Although the everyday comings and goings of these next-door neighbours is about as diverse as is possible within a city, nowhere is the crossover more companionable then when it comes to food. City workers dash from constricted offices to the welcoming environs of born-again East End boozers such as The Gun in Docklands. Lovingly brought back to life, much like the area that surrounds it, this new breed of quality gastropub is a familiar sight in this part of town. The City is

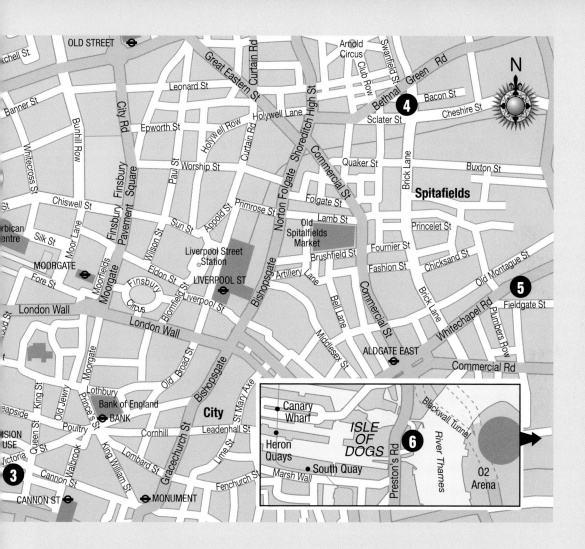

also known for its quick turnaround lunch venues, such as Sweetings. Here, first-rate food is delivered at breakneck speed to allow for the constraints of indulging in a sit-down meal during a finite break.

1. The Quality Chop House
2. Bleeding Heart Tavern
3. Sweetings
4. Beigel Bake
5. Tayyabs
6. The Gun

Beigel Bake

159 Brick Lane, E1

The reputation of this innocuous-looking bakery is such that people from every corner of the capital are aware of it and many are prepared to travel far and wide for a bag of beigels.

If it wasn't for the queues you might walk straight passed this humble looking bakery on Brick Lane, barely giving it a second glance. However, if you're in the know, you will take your place in the queue and wait patiently for your turn at the counter, where your senses will go into overdrive. The vast array of wonderful, freshly baked breads and pastries can be a bit overwhelming for the Beigel Bake novice but the homely aroma of warm bread will ensure you leave with a bag full of goodies.

The Brick Lane location might seem like an unlikely spot for a Jewish bakery but you don't have to delve too far back into the history of the East End to see why this particular establishment takes pride of place on the road and has stood the test of time. Most of the other restaurants and cafes in the nearby vicinity specialise in Asian cuisine. They cater to the area's large Bangladeshi community, as well as curry connoisseurs who travel from all over London to sample the vast selection of regional dishes on offer. Brick Lane has always been home to large immigrant populations and each successive wave of nationalities has had a major role to play in shaping the area in terms of language, cuisine, culture and infrastructure.

Beigel Bake bears the legacy of the large Jewish immigration in the East End during the late 1800s. People were fleeing from their homelands across Eastern Europe and Brick Lane was one of the cheaper areas in the city, which meant that many of the newly arrived migrants settled there. The community slowly disbanded to other parts of London but, as with other immigrants before them,

they left permanent reminders of their residence in the area. Beigel Bake remains a stalwart Jewish institution that serves traditional fare to an appreciative clientele. Members of the Jewish community can indulge their taste buds with the

BEIGEL BAKE
BRICK LANE BAKERY
o.159
OPEN 24 HOURS 7 DAYS
Tel. 071-729 0616
HOT
BEIGELS
ALL NIGHT
OPEN

authentic flavours of their ancestry, whilst hungry passers-by can stock up on quality delicacies.

Beigel Bake is a classic example of what can happen when word of mouth takes on a life of its own. The reputation of this innocuous-looking bakery is such that people from every corner of the capital are aware of it and many are prepared to

travel far and wide for a bag of beigels. The bakery is open 24 hours a day, with fresh batches of beigels coming out of the ovens at regular intervals. With its accidental position in close proximity to some of London's trendiest bars and clubs, Beigel Bake has cornered the post-clubbing market and the smell of freshly baked beigels proves too much of a temptation for hungry and weary night owls on their way home. The queue can be long at kicking out time but it moves quickly and those waiting know that they are only minutes away from beigel heaven.

If you do pay a visit to Beigel Bake and are overwhelmed by the assortment of sandwiches, fillings, cakes, pastries and buns that nudge each other for some counter space, you could join the thousands of others who opt for the bakery's signature salt beef beigel. It's a wonderfully rich and piquant snack that epitomises the historical importance and continued success of this flourishing Jewish bakery.

Bleeding Heart Tavern

Bleeding Heart Yard, EC1

The Bleeding Heart Tavern exemplifies all that is good about London restaurants. It has a broad appeal and an incredible longevity that is steeped in history but is largely a result of serving consistently good food.

If you're looking for a genuine piece of London eating and imbibing history then the Bleeding Heart Tavern is a great place to start. This popular pub and restaurant is the business lunch and dinner venue of choice for hordes of city workers during the week.

As one of the oldest pubs in London, the Tavern can stake its rightful claim to historical authenticity with a sense of pride but it is no shabby corner of nostalgia. The Tavern has evolved and expanded to cater to its patrons by including a number of eating opportunities within the cavernous building. From breakfast and bar snacks to full, formal dining, this London eating institution has stood the test of time and the annals of London life to remain a favourite with everyone who has enjoyed a meal there.

The Bleeding Heart Tavern is located in an area of London that seeps history and intrigue from every pore. Hatton Gardens is metres away and this has long been the destination of choice for every young man looking for a ring to accompany a proposal of marriage. Gray's Inn Field and Lincoln

Inn Fields are just a stone's throw further away and these bastions of British law are where barristers and judges conduct their business, and have done for hundreds of years. The name 'Bleeding Heart' is in itself a nod towards the venue's tumultuous past, standing as it has by the entrance to the yard of the same name since 1746. It is said that a jealous suitor murdered a beautiful young socialite called Lady Elizabeth Hatton in the yard in 1662. It was a frenzied attack that left her limbs ripped from her body, while her heart still pumped blood. The more romantic residents of the area adopted another, less brutal, legend. They believed that the bleeding heart belonged to a lovesick young girl who was kept locked in a room by her father for refusing to give up her lover.

Although the truth behind the name might be ambiguous, the quality of the food served in the Tavern, restaurant and bistro is far more certain. The Tavern is known for the consistency and high quality of its ingredients and meals. The menu takes the best on offer from classic French and British traditions and then adds a sprinkling of individuality to the fare. It is hearty food that has been cooked with a delicate touch and the convivial surroundings of all the dining areas make this a diverse venue that provides the answer to any number of social gathering conundrums. The wine list is superlative, as would be expected from an establishment with a large quota of city clientele but it is by no means elitist, offering something for every palate and purse and a good selection of wines by the glass, as well.

The Bleeding Heart Tavern exemplifies all that is good about London restaurants. It has a broad appeal and an incredible longevity that is steeped in history but is largely a result of serving consistently good food.

LEEDING HEART *Taver*

The Bleeding Heart Tavern
first opened its doors in 1746 when
there was one Tavern for every
five dwellings. London's brewers
produced 36 gallons of beer for
every man, woman and child &
30 distilleries made 7 million
gallons of gin to be quaffed in the
6,000 Gin Shops crammed
between the Ale houses

Some taverns boasted that their
Customers could be drunk for a penny
& dead drunk for twopence.
Some offered a back room with free
Straw where customers were laid to
sleep it off until they were able to
Carouse once more. Tobias Smollett
said that such establishments were
'seminaries of drunkenness
debauchery, extravagance &
every vice incident to human nature'

The Bleed
first opened
when the p
a licence
Sober life
In fact app
on behalf
Merchant
than beg
hoped to in
little christ
practice

The Gun

25 Coldharbour, E14

This eminently popular restaurant has demonstrated that merriment and the enjoyment of food and drink are still as popular in this tiny corner of Docklands now as they were 250 years ago.

Despite the fact that there has been a watering hole on the site of The Gun for over 250 years, the current incarnation of the pub has only been open since 2004. Since then, it has gained a fantastic reputation as a serious gastro pub, with food to rival any top-class restaurant. This is a credit to the proprietors, Tom and Ed Martin, who had a clear vision in mind about the kind of venue they wanted to create. That vision was made infinitely more difficult to realise, given that the interior of the building was gutted by a fire just a few years before the purchase and it was taken on by the brothers in its incredibly sorry state. Now fully restored to reflect its glorious past, The Gun stands proudly on the riverbank, overlooking the o2 Arena, and it has become a destination pub and dining room for the Canary Wharf after-work crowd.

The whole area is steeped in nautical history, with guns that were made in the docks being used by the Royal Navy in campaigns during the eighteenth and nineteenth centuries. Nelson himself bought a house that was just a stone's throw away from the pub so that he could easily get to the Docks and inspect the workmanship of the guns. In fact, he was a local and would often pop in for a much-needed drink on his way to or from the dockyard. Although the fervent activity of the docks has now been replaced by meandering sightseeing tours and commuter boat services, the sense of history is still fresh in the air and it's not difficult to conjure up images of ships being loaded and unloaded, stevedores

running about purposefully and sailors stepping onto dry land and straight into the pub for a drink.

Whilst those thirsty sailors might not have appreciated the thought that has gone into the regeneration of this beautiful and historically important old building and the new lease of life that has been breathed into the area, the customers certainly do. No detail has been overlooked in the meticulous refit and this extends to the well thought out menu. With a serious nod of appreciation towards the bounty of the sea, there is also a good selection of hearty meat options and each final dish is a carefully considered summation of its individual component parts. The restaurant

is located in the bar area so the atmosphere is relaxed and informal, although the food could never be described as pub grub.

The Gun is proof that history can reinvent itself, that crumbling old buildings can be given a new lease of life and that a seriously good restaurant can earn an established reputation in very little time. This eminently popular restaurant has demonstrated that merriment and the enjoyment of food and drink are still as popular in this tiny corner of Docklands now as they were 250 years ago. With banking and publishing having taken over from gun making and smuggling, it's fascinating to see a piece of history literally brought back to life.

The Quality Chop House

92-94 Farringdon Road, EC1

The Quality Chop House has withstood the changing tides of culinary fads and trends and has remained a constant presence in Clerkenwell, dishing up good-value fare to its broad range of customers.

There aren't many London restaurants that can claim to have been dishing up dinner from the same premises, under the same name, since the 1870s. The Grade II Listed building was designed by Sir Roland Plumbe who, at the time, was a revolutionary architect. He believed in trying to alleviate social malady through good building design. In many ways, the concept of The Quality Chop House was much the same but replacing buildings with food. The no-nonsense menu was brief and simple with the one aim of filling tummies with nutritious food for very little money.

Chop Houses were a common sight across London in the nineteenth century. They provided a hospitable environment in which to enjoy a hearty meal and a jug of beer. They were essentially working class restaurants and were also known as 'eating houses', a utilitarian name that aptly described the no-frills approach to the food. As other budget restaurants came on the scene, chop houses fell by the wayside but the idea of good quality meat cuts, simply presented and served, is once again coming back into favour and the chop house is seeing something of a resurgence. The Quality Chop House has withstood the changing tides of culinary fads and trends and has remained a constant presence in Clerkenwell, dishing up good-value fare to its broad range of customers. From struggling

The Quality Cho...

Dining and Tea...

students, hungry tradesmen and office workers to theatre-goers and party people, the reliable menu attracts people from all walks of life.

Despite a major refurbishment in the 1980s, The Quality Chop House has changed little in its long and fascinating history. Even in its modernisation, the interior was sympathetically restored and remained in keeping with its Victorian ancestry. Simple oak tables and bench seating accommodate the customers while the clean lines of the tiled floor and the elegant lighting and mirrors add just enough character and warmth to create a more personable dining environment than would have been in evidence 140 years ago. The food is reassuringly simple and hearty: there are no convoluted descriptions or ambiguous sounding ingredients. You can picture your plate of food with incredible accuracy while you read the menu and there are no unexpected surprises when the plate arrives. Everything is as you hoped it would be, but the taste surpasses your expectations.

The recipes are largely timeless classics that have been enjoyed by the British working classes for generations. Of course, some adjustments have been made to account for changing palates and the availability of more ingredients. After all, there have to be some benefits to being over 100 years further along the culinary timeline. However, much of the food still harks back to the original Victorian Chop House menu and the staples of the classic British cookbook. You'll find devilled kidneys, steak and kidney pie and, of course, chops. A good selection of wine and beer ensures that this basic fare can be enjoyed at a leisurely pace, although the unforgiving wooden benches have been known to put an end to many a lingering dinner.

Sweetings

39 Queen Victoria Street, EC4

Sweetings is a London classic and a City favourite. It offers everything that a ravenous, time-pressed worker could ask for from a restaurant and it's not afraid to set its own agenda.

Having first opened to the paying public in 1889, Sweetings can rightfully claim to be one of London's oldest restaurants. In fact, if you walk through the doors today, you will be greeted by much the same ambience and surroundings as you would in the late nineteenth century. Essentially a City worker's lunch venue, this traditional fish restaurant holds very much to its old-school principles and it hasn't let the advances of the modern world hold too much sway over how it operates. A prime example is that, until relatively recently, Sweetings didn't accept credit cards. One would assume that a City banker wouldn't dream of leaving home without a pocketful of bank notes but this rather draconian cash-only payment system undoubtedly caught out many diners.

There are a number of other eccentricities that ensure Sweetings continues to break the mould of the perceived universal practises of modern restaurants. For one, it doesn't take bookings – not that this is a problem in terms of ensuring the place is full. Turn up after midday on any given weekday and you'll find yourself in an already substantial queue to be seated. And, if you were thinking of saving yourself for dinner, then you might need to make alternative arrangements: Sweetings is only open for lunch and it is only open during the week. Although this may sound absurd in terms of dining out in metropolitan London, it isn't actually all that unusual in the City. Although many pubs and restaurants do now open for evening service, a number of the more traditional establishments shut their doors once the last lunchtime diners have left

on a Friday afternoon and they don't open them again until Monday. The City might be a heaving mass of hungry workers with money to burn during the day and during the week, but much of it is deserted after dark and all weekend. It simply didn't make economic sense for establishments to stay open once the bankers had caught the train home.

With regards to the fare that it serves, once again Sweetings sticks like glue to tradition. Having only passed through a handful of owners during its

existence, it has managed to avoid the trappings and trimmings of ultra modern cuisine. It prides itself on the quality of its menu and the fact that it almost exclusively adheres to Great British fish and seafood classics such as potted shrimp, smoked haddock, and fish pie. It is simply prepared, simply presented food that exceeds expectations.

The menu is refreshingly free of superfluous adjectives and pointless garni descriptions and instead it highlights the key ingredients of the dish. A selection of sticky, steamed and baked puds harks back to the restaurant's Victorian era and offers the ultimate comfort food in a bowl. While the slick city bars slide plates of minimalist nibbles to their clientele, Sweetings fills their stomachs with hearty, homemade food that will see them through the afternoon and the long commute home. However,

despite going off the scale when it comes to old-fashioned comfort food, Sweetings makes no bones about the fact that it doesn't want its diners to dawdle: enjoy, indulge and savour by all means but it certainly doesn't encourage any lingering at the dining table once the plates have been cleared away. With such a short opportunity to fill the cash tills, all eyes are on the clock, as the long, raised tables are swiftly cleared and the next batch of bankers are ushered in. Sweetings has deliberately kept coffee off the menu and the wooden bar stools do little to inspire the diner to sit back and slowly digest their jam roly poly.

Sweetings is a London classic and a City favourite. It offers everything that a ravenous, time-pressed worker could ask for from a restaurant and it's not afraid to set its own agenda.

Tayyabs

83 Fieldgate Street, E1

Tayyabs has clearly got a winning formula and its reputation continues to draw in new customers, as well as ensuring its regulars return to eat there again

Tayyabs has been busy building up its stellar reputation since it first opened as a small café in 1975. The restaurant was borne out of necessity in an area populated by Pakistani immigrant workers looking for an authentic taste of home at a reasonable price. Men would often be living in shared accommodation without the time or facilities to cook substantial meals and it didn't take long for news of the café to spread and the tables to be full of appreciative diners.

The Tayyab family were originally from Pakistani Punjab and the restaurant reflects the classic flavours of the region with an emphasis on spiced meat, dhals and tandoor-baked breads. As the café continued to increase in popularity, the family took over a pub that was next door and they expanded the business to cater for an ever-expanding clientele. As word spread, the Asian regulars were joined by non-Asian curry enthusiasts, many of whom had become disillusioned by the influx of inferior restaurants on neighbouring Brick Lane. The philosophy at Tayyabs has remained the same as when the first café was founded and that is to provide wholesome food in a convivial atmosphere

at reasonable prices. They haven't embraced the nouvelle curry fetish and jumped-up price list of many of their contemporaries and instead they have kept the food authentic and the pricing low. This has ensured the constant stream of customers and the long list of accolades that the restaurant enjoys.

Despite the popularity of the restaurant, Tayyabs is dedicated to excellent customer service and food is served quickly and efficiently. The waiters are highly skilled and this in itself is something of a rarity in many restaurants. Food is freshly prepared, piping hot and inviting, with a wealth of aromas emanating from the plate, and a burst of wonderful flavours on the palate. Tayyabs offers that rare combination of curry comfort food that combines authenticity, quality and great value for money. It is a family-run business that has stood the test of time and continues to produce consistently good food. This isn't haute cuisine, it isn't fancy cooking in a flashy setting; it's far more than that. This is honest, home-cooked food with the primary objective of giving people pleasure. Tayyabs has clearly got a winning formula and its reputation continues to draw in new customers, as well as ensuring its regulars return to eat there again and again. Popularity hasn't resulted in it resting on its laurels and relying on word-of-mouth trade. As everyone knows, reputations can be made and destroyed in quick succession and the food must always be deserving of the compliments it receives. At Tayyabs, the queues are inevitably here to stay as the restaurant reconfirms its solid reputation with every visit. People have no qualms about queuing for a good thing and the long line outside Tayyabs speaks for itself

WATERLOO AND STRAND

Waterloo and Strand sit directly opposite each other over the River Thames. They are both gateways to theatrical London with the Strand heralding the southernmost border of Covent Garden and the bustling theatre district of London. A short boat ride away, Waterloo is home to the likes of the National Theatre, the Royal Festival Hall and The Old Vic. This has undoubtedly had an impact on the nature of the restaurants that serve this area but, whilst the Strand has always exalted in its eminent social and culinary status with establishments such as The Savoy and Simpson's-in-the-Strand attracting moneyed culture vultures, Waterloo has maintained a grittier and more urban feel. Recently, major regeneration has spruced up the area but stalwarts such as Meson Don Felipe have watched indifferent as there has always been a queue outside the door of this much-loved tapas joint.

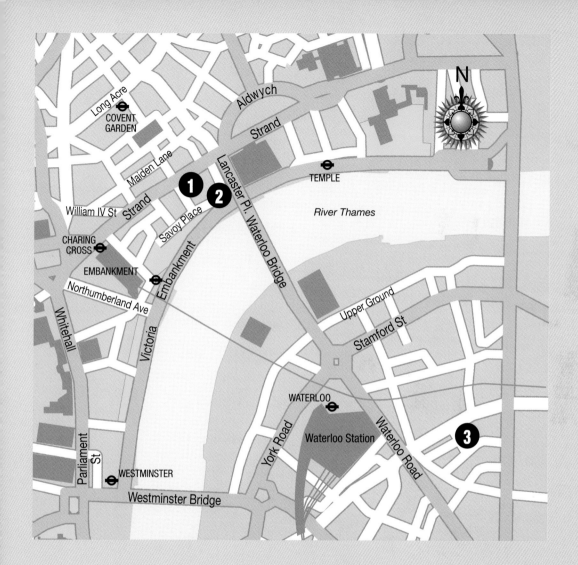

1. Simpsons-in-the-strand
2. The Savoy
3. Meson Don Felipe

Meson Don Felipe

53 The Cut, SE1

Meson Don Felipe is a little corner of Spain in the heart of Waterloo. The atmosphere is charged and buzzing, the welcome is always warm and there's even a flamenco guitarist.

This intimate Waterloo tapas bar is a perennial favourite with the local after-work crowd, as well as being a popular spot for friends meeting up in town for a gossip accompanied by a constant selection of delicious little snacks. From the outside, you might barely register that you are strolling past a restaurant, as the high windows with metal trellising do little to convey the atmosphere inside. However, this hasn't put too many people off and, once discovered, this gem of a restaurant is oft revisited by its glut of happy customers.

Meson Don Felipe is a little corner of Spain in the heart of Waterloo. Although much has changed around this area over the last ten years or so, the tapas bar has held pride of place on its corner from the days when Waterloo was little more than a thoroughfare. Regeneration has seen a huge influx of gastro pubs, bars and cafes along The Cut and other roads in the immediate vicinity of Waterloo station and there are now a couple of other tapas restaurants vying for trade. However they seem to have had little or no impact on the popularity of this much-beloved dining room.

For regulars – or hungry passers-by who choose to ignore the unassuming exterior and plunge through the front door – the reward is great. Once inside, there's a genuine feeling of having been transplanted to the Continent and the lack of vista onto the outside world only adds to the ambience. On busy nights – which tend to be most nights – the buzz of conversation from the diners and the clink of countless dishes being stacked and ferried to and from the kitchen can reach epic proportions. But once you have found sufficient space to squeeze into and you've ordered some drinks, you are soon merging into the foray and you can soak up the atmosphere with abandon.

The layout of the restaurant is hectic to say the least. Tables jostle for space all around the outer walls whilst the centre of the room is taken up by a huge bar area, where tapas can be enjoyed the traditional way; sitting up with a drink and a couple of plates of nibbles to wash it down. There never seems to be a spare table and if you haven't

booked you might get looks of surprise from the waiting staff as they and you glance around the packed restaurant. However, the tardis-like space can be deceiving and the staff can work miracles with a few shuffles of a table or the relocation of a couple of chairs.

The menu is a tried-and-tested selection of Anglo-friendly tapas, authentic but definitely tailored to British diners. Service is quick, friendly and efficient and the whole experience is based around the concept of sharing food: picking and choosing a number of dishes that whet your appetite and having the opportunity to try them all. Patatas bravas, tortilla and deep-fried mushrooms are just some of the favourites on offer and, although there is little in the way of contemporary twists on the food, that's not what Meson Don Felipe is about. There are

plenty of ûbuer cool tapas joints in London that offer a high-end take on this classic Spanish cusine. This particular restaurant keeps it simple and relies on the consistent preparation of the old-school dishes on which it built its reputation.

Meson Don Felipe offers so much more than just plates of food. The atmosphere is charged and buzzing, the welcome is always warm and there's even a flamenco guitarist who tries to make his music heard above the hum of the restaurant. The place is so busy that even he doesn't get his own space. Instead, he climbs up to a tiny platform above the door to the kitchen and balances precariously on an old chair, surveying the comings and goings below while he strums on his guitar.

The Savoy

Strand, WC2

The Savoy Grill has succeeded in appealing to a wide range of diners by offering a menu that is both diverse yet coherent and food that is exquisitely cooked and beautifully presented.

The Savoy stands proud on the Strand in London's West End and has been providing bed and board since it opened in 1889. The site had been razed by a huge fire in 1864 and was bought by Richard D'Oyly Carte, having lain empty for years. He was looking for a venue on which to build a new theatre where he could showcase his Gilbert and Sullivan productions. As a bit of a jack of all trades, D'Oyly Carte had a long list of occupations trailing his name, hotelier being just one of them. Obviously believing that hotels and theatres made natural bedfellows, he also built The Savoy hotel. He employed César Ritz as the Hotel Manager and it would seem that The Savoy was a good training ground, as he went on to build his own hotel empire.

The Savoy was the place to be seen throughout the late nineteenth and early twentieth century and indeed it is still considered to be one of the finest and most famous hotels in the city. A veritable roll call of the rich and famous have stayed at the hotel over the years, sipped cocktails in the famous American Bar and had dinner in the restaurant. The Savoy Grill has always been something of a career objective for top chefs, symbolising as it does the absolute pinnacle of

their craft. This tradition goes right back to the early years of the restaurant when the famous chef, Auguste Escoffier, took the reins in the kitchen. Escoffier was the equivalent to today's celebrity chefs and people would travel from far and wide to dine in the Savoy Grill and sample the great man's food.

A succession of talented and creative chefs have followed in Escoffier's footsteps to maintain the reputation of the Savoy Grill and to ensure that the quality of the food and the menu selection is in keeping with the quality of the hotel.

The Savoy Grill has succeeded in appealing to a wide range of diners by offering a menu that is both diverse yet coherent and food that is exquisitely cooked and beautifully presented. To its credit, it has managed to maintain a unique style, whilst also engaging the taste buds of diners from all over the world. As a hotel restaurant, the tastes of the guests must be of paramount importance and it is vital to ensure their satisfaction from a meal. However, non-resident patronage is also important to the continued success of the restaurant and, as such, the menu has to work on a number of different levels, meeting the culinary requirements of a diverse range of diners. By succeeding on both fronts, the Savoy Grill has lasted where many other restaurants have failed and it remains a credit to the hotel.

Over the years the original Edwardian style of the hotel has been tweaked and changed to reflect more modern design styles and also to accommodate modern hotel facilities. Art Deco remained a big theme throughout the hotel but the owners felt there was a lack of definition and coherence. To remedy the situation, the Savoy shut its doors at the end of 2007 to begin a huge programme of modernisation and refurbishment. This level of commitment to the continuation of the great name of the hotel shows that it intends to be welcoming guests for a long time to come.

Simpsons-in-the-Strand

100 Strand, WC2

Simpsons-in-the-Strand provides an ongoing reminder of the significance of food in the history of London.

This wonderfully ornate dining room offers a rare glimpse into the culinary history of London. The atmospheric interior makes it easy to conjure up tableaux of cherry-faced, whiskered gentlemen clinking their glasses over a roast beef dinner whilst discussing important matters of the day. Indeed, such luminaries as Charles Dickens and William Gladstone have graced Simpsons with their presence and have enjoyed platters of great British food.

The décor might have been touched up and the dress code modernised but, in effect, a meal at this British dining institution isn't too far removed from the experience enjoyed by diners over 100 years ago. The same principles of classic British food still apply and the roast beef signature dish still takes pride of place on the menu and is very much in demand. The tradition of bringing the silver-domed serving trolleys to the table is one that was instigated when the venue took its first tentative steps towards becoming a restaurant. It was originally a chess club but as chess can be unpredictable in terms of the length of each game, it was decided to bring food to the players' tables. This meant that their game didn't need to be interrupted by growling stomachs and the need to wander off in search

of a meal. If you order roast beef in Simpsons today, your meal will arrive in exactly the same way and it adds a real sense of occasion to dinner when the food is ceremoniously wheeled through the restaurant to your table.

Simpsons has become known for its excellent execution of the British culinary classics and there has been little tampering with these dishes over the years. The menu is distinctly British and the reputation of the restaurant has been built around its dedication to serving the best of British to its patrons. Fresh, seasonal ingredients are in abundance on the menu and this has always been the case. Although seasonality has become a major issue for restaurants in more recent years, with many now making a fuss about their use of home grown produce, Simpsons has been quietly adhering to this principle since it first opened.

It has a loyal customer base and these regular diners rely on the consistency and quality of the food, as well as the personable service that Simpsons provides. It is a homely restaurant and yet it still manages to exude an air of sophistication and a level of pampering that matches the luxurious comfort food that it serves its patrons.

Simpsons-in-the-Strand provides an ongoing reminder of the significance of food in the history of London. Eras can be defined by the existence of certain restaurants and different styles of food that have been fashionable over the years. Simpsons harks back to a bygone age and, in that respect, it could be said to be an anachronism. However, its relevance in today's culinary environment is certified by its continued popularity and it holds it head high as one of London's classic restaurants.

ADDRESSES

SOHO AND FRITZROVIA

Andrew Edmunds
46 Lexington Street, W1F 0LW
TUBE: Oxford Circus

Bar Italia
22 Frith Street, W1D 4RP
www.baritaliasoho.co.uk
TUBE: Tottenham Court Road, Leicester Square

The French House
49 Dean Street, W1D 5BG
www.frenchhousesoho.com
TUBE: Leicester Square

The Gay Hussar
2 Greek Street, W1B 4NB
www.gayhussar.co.uk
TUBE: Tottenham Court Road

Kettner's
29 Romilly Street, W1D 5HP
www.kettners.com
TUBE: Leicester Square

The Langham
1c Portland Place, W1B 1JA
www.langhamhotels.co.uk
TUBE: Oxford Circus

Maison Bertaux
28 Greek Street, W1D 5DQ
www.maisonbertaux.com
TUBE: Leicester Square

Patisserie Valerie
44 Old Compton Street, W1D 4TY
www.patisserie-valerie.co.uk
TUBE: Leicester Square

PICCADILLY

Bentley's Oyster Bar and Grill
11-15 Swallow Street, W1B 4DG
www.bentleys.org
TUBE: Piccadilly Circus

Criterion
224 Piccadilly, W1J 9HP
www.criterionrestaurant.com
TUBE: Piccadilly Circus

Fortnum and Mason
181 Piccadilly, W1A 1ER
www.fortnumandmason.com
TUBE: Green Park

Langan's Brasserie
Stratton Street, W1J 8LB
www.langansrestaurants.co.uk
TUBE: Green Park

The Ritz
150 Piccadilly, W1J 9BR
www.theritzlondon.com
TUBE: Green Park

MAYFAIR, ST JAMES AND KNIGHTSBRIDGE

Claridge's
Brook Street, W1K 4HR
www.claridges.co.uk
TUBE: Bond Street

The Connaught
Carlos Place, W1K 2AL
www.the-connaught.co.uk
TUBE: Bond Street

The Dorchester
Park Lane, W1K 1QA
www.thedorchester.com
TUBE: Hyde Park Corner

Langtry's
21 Pont Street, SW1X 9SG
www.langtrysrestaurant.com
TUBE: Knightsbridge

Le Gavroche
43 Upper Brook Street, W1K 7QR
www.le-gavroche.co.uk
TUBE: Marble Arch

Rowley's
113 Jermyn Street, SW1Y 6HJ
www.rowleys.co.uk
TUBE: Piccadilly Circus

Veeraswamy
Victory House, 99 Regent Street, W1B 4RS
www.veeraswamy.com
TUBE: Piccadilly Circus

Wiltons
55 Jermyn Street, SW1Y 6LX
www.wiltons.co.uk
TUBE: Green Park

The Wolseley
160 Piccadilly, W1J 9EB
www.thewolseley.com
TUBE: Green Park

COVENT GARDEN

The Ivy
1-5 West Street, WC2H 9NQ
www.the-ivy.co.uk
TUBE: Leicester Square

J. Sheekey
28-34 St Martin's Court, WC2N 4AL
www.j-sheekey.co.uk
TUBE: Leicester Square

Mon Plaisir

19-21 Monmouth Street, WC2H 9DD

www.monplaisir.co.uk

TUBE: Covent Garden

Punjab

80 Neal Street, WC2H 9PA

www.punjab.co.uk

TUBE: Covent Garden

The Rock and Sole Plaice

47 Endell Street, WC2H 9AJ

TUBE: Covent Garden

Rules

35 Maiden Lane, WC2E 7LB

www.rules.co.uk

TUBE: Charring Cross, Covent Garden

SOUTH LONDON

Arments

7&9 Westmoreland Road, SE17 2AX

www.armentspieandmash.com

TUBE: Elephant and Castle, London Bridge

Beauberry House

Gallery Road, SE21 7AB

www.beauberryhouse.co.uk

RAIL: West Dulwich

M. Manze

87 Tower Bridge Road, SE1 4TW

www.manze.co.uk

TUBE: Borough

EAST LONDON AND THE CITY

Beigel Bake

159 Brick Lane, E1 6SB

TUBE: Liverpool Street

Bleeding Heart Tavern

Bleeding Heart Yard, Off Greville Street, EC1N 8SJ

www.bleedingheart.co.uk

TUBE: Farringdon

The Gun

25 Coldharbour, E14 9NS

www.thegundocklands.com

TUBE: Canary Wharf

The Quality Chop House
94 Farringdon Road, EC1R 3EA
www.qualitychophouse.co.uk
TUBE: Farringdon

Sweetings
39 Queen Victoria Street, EC4N 4SA
TUBE: Mansion House

Tayyabs
83 Fieldgate Street, E1 1JU
www.tayyabs.co.uk
TUBE: Whitechapel

WATERLOO AND STRAND

Meson Don Felipe
53 The Cut, SE1 8LF
www.mesondonfelipe.com
TUBE: Waterloo, Southwark

The Savoy
Strand, WC2R 0EU
www.the-savoy.com
TUBE: Charring Cross

Simpsons-in-the-Strand
100 Strand, WC2R 0EW
www.simpsonsinthestrand.co.uk
TUBE: Charring Cross

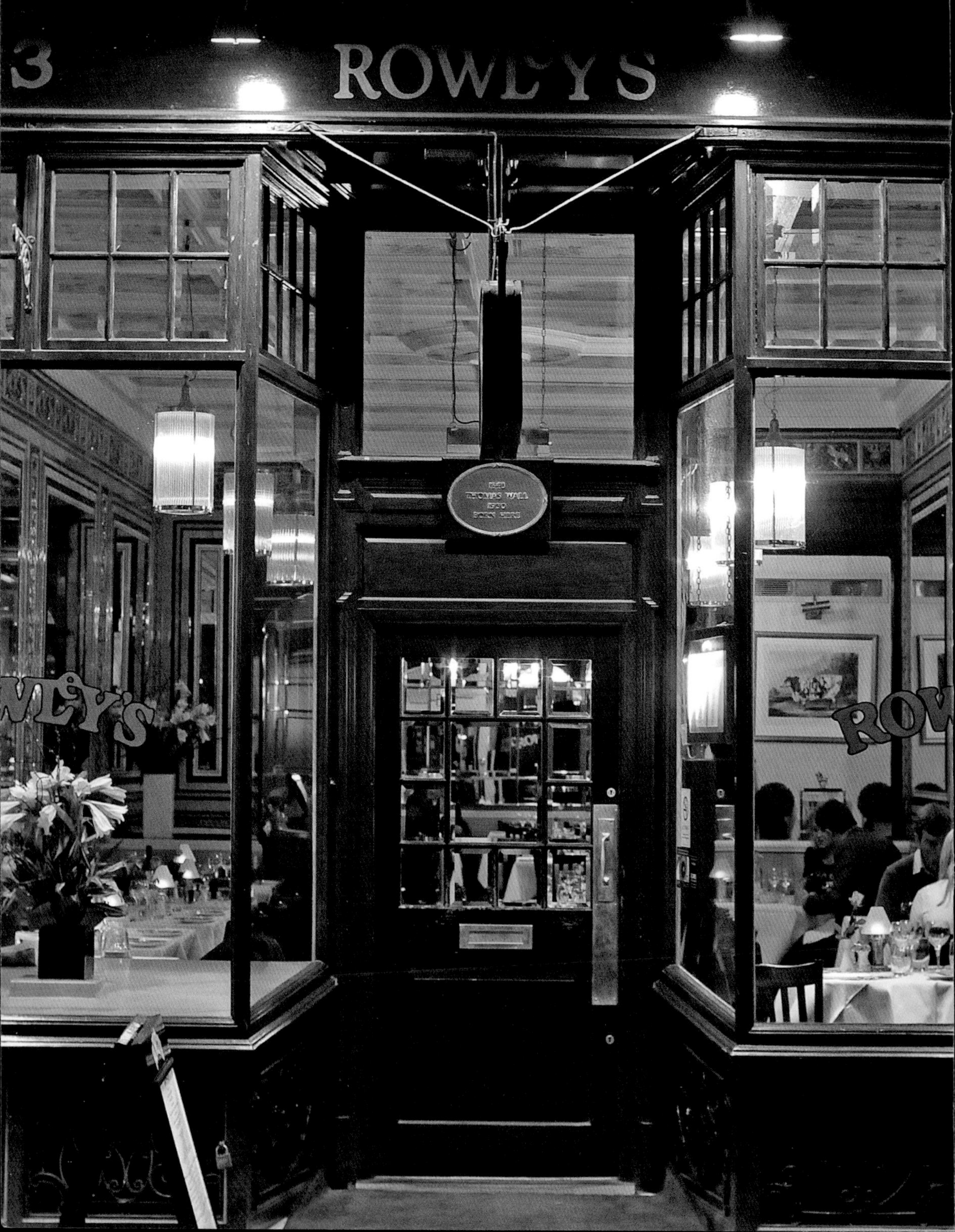
ROWLEYS